The Politics of Energy

THE POLITICS
OF ENERGY

BARRY COMMONER

Alfred A. Knopf   *New York*   1979

THIS IS A BORZOI BOOK
PUBLISHED BY ALFRED A. KNOPF, INC.

Portions of this book have previously appeared in *The New Yorker*.

Library of Congress Cataloging in Publication Data

Commoner, Barry, [date]
  The politics of energy.

  Includes index.
  1. Energy policy—United States. I. Title.
HD9502.U52C654 333.7   79-7325
ISBN 0-394-50800-9
ISBN 0-394-73808-X pbk.

Manufactured in the United States of America

FIRST EDITION

Contents

Prologue

Imagine that somewhere in outer space there are beings so much more advanced than ourselves that they have learned how to eavesdrop, from many light-years away, on earthly communications. Suppose, too, that their marvelous galactic listening device first began receiving news from the United States a little over two years ago, let us say on April 18, 1977, the day on which President Jimmy Carter presented his National Energy Plan to the nation. What will these distant listeners now know about the United States?

On April 18, they heard Jimmy Carter broadcast a warning that the country was "running out of gas and oil," so that, forced to depend increasingly on oil imports, "we will live in fear of embargoes" that would threaten "an economic, social and political crisis." They heard the President call for a campaign to solve the energy crisis that would amount to the "moral equivalent of war."

In the months that followed, there was news of the country's response to the President's urgent call. The immediate reaction was good. Commentators praised the President's strong initiative; the administration's energy bills went through the legislative machinery with hardly a hitch; they were passed with record speed in the House of Representatives. The alien listeners must have been impressed with the vigor and efficiency of American society.

Then the messages became confused. In the Senate, Carter's Plan was dismembered, and by the end of the year there was little left of it, as the legislators took off for the holidays, and the intergalactic airwaves were full of Christmas carols instead of political talk. With the New Year the confusion turned into chaos. The administration's position changed: whereas a few months before, messages from the White House spoke of energy conservation as the "cornerstone" of the Plan, now they spoke of raising the price of natural gas (through deregulation) as the Plan's "centerpiece." While earlier Carter called nuclear power the energy source of "last resort," now, according to Secretary of Energy James R. Schlesinger, nuclear power was "enshrined in the President's program." Finally, an energy bill was passed that the *Wall Street Journal* said "bears only a faint resemblance to President Carter's original proposals." But the White House called it a victory.

That was in October 1978. Within a month most of the talk was not about energy but inflation. While the White House and its supporters in Congress originally favored higher energy prices, now they complained bitterly that the rising price of oil was inflationary and threatened an economic depression. Inflation, the President said, was the country's most serious problem, and to fight it government costs must be cut. His new budget proposed cuts in health, job programs, and housing—and an increase in military expenditures. There were many complaints that these cuts would hurt the poor, minorities, older people, and the cities generally. But *The New York Times* gave the President editorial support for "a policy of pain," and the columnist George F. Will proposed to make the pain acceptable by spreading it around. He said, "Perhaps the way to persuade an interest group that it does not have a special grievance is to generalize grief . . . to democratize disappointment." The cover of *Newsweek* magazine proclaimed the start of a new era: "The Politics of Austerity." The alien listeners' opinion of the strength of American society must have suffered a sharp decline.

By February 1979 the intergalactic airwaves carried dire new messages. The people of Iran had overthrown their monarch, the Shah, and in the process stopped oil production; when it resumed the price was higher. Although only 2.5 percent of U.S. oil comes from Iran, this precipitated a series of economic and political reactions: oil companies restricted fuel supplies and airlines began to cancel flights; the government made plans to ration gasoline; there was a sense of crisis in the air. Iran's action, officials warned, was a reminder of how much the U.S. depends on Middle Eastern oil; defense officials —and a flight of military planes—paid a visit to Saudi Arabia, where much of our imported oil comes from. A "senior treasury official" ominously asserted that "a crisis creates the opportunity to get something done that is otherwise politically unfeasible."

Soon the intercepted messages began to explain what some of these "otherwise politically unfeasible" actions might be. Although in the aftermath of the disastrous war in Vietnam the country had seemed glad to be at peace, now some belligerent voices were heard. Washington *Post* columnist David Broder said: "It is time for the United States to show the flag, and Carter to show some backbone." Marvin Stone, editor of *U.S. News & World Report,* said: "The world must be convinced that we are willing to use our strength where we must. This is hard. This is dangerous. But it is a dangerous world."

Then, in March 1979, the administration decided to send arms and "instructors" to Yemen Arab Republic (North Yemen), a desert country about the size of North Dakota that produces little beyond a few crops, because, as Representative Lee Hamilton (Dem., Ind.) put it, "We are all of a sudden being told our national interest is involved." North Yemen shares borders with Saudi Arabia and South Yemen, an "unfriendly" country. During Congressional hearings on this action, the following exchange took place:

Representative Lee Hamilton: Is the United States prepared to go to war to protect Saudi oil?

William R. Crawford (Deputy Assistant Secretary of State for Near Eastern and South Asian Affairs): We do regard the integrity and the maintenance of the integrity of the kingdom of Saudi Arabia as vital to American interests in the Middle East, and we would—should be prepared to act in implementation of that consideration.

Hamilton: I want you to know, Mr. Crawford . . . that I consider that response an affirmative answer to my question. Would you so interpret it?

Crawford: I believe so; yes.

Then on March 28 there was more bad news: an accident at the Three Mile Island Nuclear Power Plant near Harrisburg, Pennsylvania, where the failure of a pump triggered a series of malfunctions which turned that supposedly benign source of electricity into a frightening threat to the health and safety of hundreds of thousands of people. But the President continued to insist that we must rely on nuclear power—that despite its risks it was an essential part of the nation's supply of energy.

All this might make sense to our galactic eavesdroppers, for they have no way of knowing, from the intercepted messages, that there are facts which contradict what they have heard. The facts are these: that, despite our dependence on imports, there is enough oil and natural gas, under the ground in the United States, to meet our needs for years to come; that the problem with relying on these fuels is that they become more and more costly as they are depleted—and that their rising price has become a major cause of inflation; that the solution to the energy crisis is not a larger military budget or a war in the Middle East, but a transition to a source that is plentiful, renewable, and stable in price—solar energy; that the transition to solar energy can begin at once; that we could, for example, easily make up for any shortage of fuel from Iran by producing a solar fuel—alcohol made from our own grain crops—a measure that could help the farmers' income, control gasoline prices, and keep inflation in check; that a solar transition, begun now, would end the need for new nuclear power plants and gradually phase out the existing ones; and that the solar transition would solve not only the energy crisis, but the economic crisis as well, for it would improve the efficiency of production, stimulate the economy, and reveal as counterfeit the notion that the United States, the richest country in human history, must enter an age of austerity.

The point of this parable is this: Like the galactic eavesdroppers, we ourselves are alien to these facts. Like the listeners in space, the people of the United States have been given only scraps of contradictory information about the energy crisis and are largely unaware of the facts that could explain what is going on. For a while the confusion was tolerable, and most people believed that if the National Energy Act seemed to do no good, at least it would do no harm. But now we can see that in its frustration over energy the country may be persuaded to accept higher oil prices that would aggravate inflation; gasoline rationing that would force the poor to buy ration stamps from the rich; cuts in social services in favor of a larger military budget; and the draft. We can now see that the confusion over energy is not harmless, but very dangerous, and that the greatest danger is that in the midst of the confusion, the United States may be conned into converting the "moral equivalent of war" into a real war.

What we now need is clarity, a sense of what is really happening, where the energy crisis is taking us, and what can be done to solve it. This book is an effort in that direction.

The Politics of Energy

1

THE NATIONAL ENERGY PLAN:
The Politics of Confusion

On the evening of April 18, 1977, President Jimmy Carter made his first major policy speech to the nation. It was an impressive performance. Speaking in somber tones, Mr. Carter seemed to personify the seriousness of the subject. "Tonight," he said, "I want to have an unpleasant talk with you about a problem unprecedented in our history. With the exception of preventing war, this is the greatest challenge our country will face in our lifetime. The energy crisis has not yet overwhelmed us, but it will if we do not act quickly. . . . Our decision about energy will test the character of the American people and the ability of the President and the Congress to govern. This difficult effort will be the 'moral equivalent of war.' "

Mr. Carter explained why the problem was so serious. He pointed out that the United States now relies on oil and natural gas for about three-fourths of the energy that runs our economy. But, he said, "we are now running out of gas and oil." Because, according to Mr. Carter, domestic production of oil and natural gas cannot be increased and the demand for energy is expected to rise by a third before 1985, if nothing is done about it we will be forced to import more and more increasingly expensive oil. As a result, "We will live in fear of embargoes. We could endanger our freedom as a sovereign nation to act in foreign affairs. . . . We will feel mounting pressure to plunder the environment. We will have a crash program to build more nuclear plants, strip-mine and burn more coal and drill more offshore wells. . . . Inflation will soar, production will go down, people will lose their jobs. . . . If we fail to act soon, we will face an economic, social and political crisis that will threaten our free institutions."

The answer to all these threats, the President said, was the National Energy Plan. On January 20, Inauguration Day, Mr. Carter had ordered a White House staff headed by Dr. James R. Schlesinger to produce such a plan. They were given ninety days for the task, and completed it exactly on time. On April 20 Mr. Carter formally presented the Plan to a joint session of Congress. Simultaneously the White House issued a detailed *Fact Sheet* about it. According to the *Fact Sheet,* the Plan was governed by ten fundamental principles; it was designed to achieve six major goals; it comprised ten major programs, each subdivided into numerous detailed proposals. The conservation program alone listed nineteen proposed measures for saving energy.

The Plan's goals were simple, but the means of achieving them were very complex. For example, to accomplish the main goal—cutting oil imports in half—intricate, circuitous methods were proposed. First, it was argued that since domestic production of oil and natural gas could not be increased and only part of the demand for oil could be met by switching to coal, the main task was to reduce demand, especially in transportation, which accounts for about a fourth of U.S. oil consumption. The direct ways of cutting fuel consumption that the Plan proposed were relatively limited: a national 55-mile-per-hour highway speed limit and automobile and truck fuel-efficiency standards. Most of the measures were oblique, designed to manipulate rather than to direct or persuade. Instead of appealing explicitly to the importance of conserving energy, they sought to exploit economic self-interest, using higher taxes as the stick and tax rebates as the carrot. Gas-guzzling automobiles would be heavily taxed, while people who bought fuel-efficient cars would receive tax rebates. If the public did not respond sufficiently to these economic stimuli and failed to cut gasoline consumption to within one percent of a gradually changing annual target, a heavier club would be used—an additional tax would be imposed on gasoline.

As a result of these measures, poor people, who use a large part of their budget for energy-consuming necessities such as getting to and from work, would carry a particularly large part of the financial burden. But this would violate the Plan's fifth principle, which calls for "equal sacrifices from every region, every class of people." To meet this difficulty the Plan also provided that the taxes would "be rebated to the American people progressively through the Federal income tax system and by direct payments to people who do not pay taxes." And since reduced gasoline consumption would cut the states' income from their own gasoline taxes, state highway maintenance funds (which depend on these taxes) would be supplemented by funds from the Federal Highway Trust Fund.

These measures reflect the Plan's basic strategy of using higher prices to cut oil and natural gas consumption. By raising the price of domestic oil and natural gas to meet that of the most costly fuel—oil on the world market—the domestic fuels would be priced at their "replacement cost." This was supposed to teach people the true value of energy and persuade them to use it less wastefully. To this end the Plan would gradually increase the controlled price of domestic oil until it reached the price of world oil, and thereafter it would keep pace with that price.

But again there were complications. If this rule were applied to existing domestic oil resources, the oil companies would reap an undeserved windfall profit—another violation of the Plan's fifth principle ("we will not let the energy companies profiteer"). So the relaxed price was to be applied only to newly discovered oil. However, it is always possible to drill a new well into an old, previously discovered oil field. To block that gambit, newly discovered oil was defined as "oil from a well drilled more than 2½ miles from an existing onshore well as of April 20, 1977, or more than 1,000 feet deeper than any well within any 2½ mile radius."

To help bring the price of domestic oil up to the level of world prices, the Plan also included a "crude oil equalization tax," which would be applied to every barrel of domestic oil as it left the ground. The tax would be imposed in increments over a three-year period and would thereafter increase with the rising cost of world oil. But, recognizing that any fuel tax is regressive (high fuel prices have their largest effect on the cost of life's necessities, such as food, clothing, and housing, and therefore disproportionately burden poor people), the Plan proposed to rebate this tax money as well. Taxpayers would receive their rebate through reduced income tax withholding. People who were too poor to pay an income tax would get their rebates by a more circuitous route: by applying to one of the state agencies that distribute welfare funds. One of the Plan's major goals was to increase the use of coal, as a replacement for oil and natural gas. Again the proposed actions were indirect and complex, using taxation as the tool. In order to encourage the substitution of coal, the Plan included a series of restrictions on the use of oil and natural gas in new industrial and power plant boilers. But since increased coal burning would intensify air pollution, the Plan also required the installation of the best available control technology in all new coal-fired plants. This was a problematic attempt to balance intensified use of coal—that and nuclear power being the energy sources most hazardous to the environment—against the importance of the Plan's third principle: "We must protect the environment."

In dealing with the question of nuclear power, the Plan intruded not only into pollution problems but also into the portentous problems of nuclear war. Because the expanded use of plutonium (which can fairly easily be made into a nuclear bomb) would tend to proliferate these weapons and intensify the already dangerous capability for nuclear war, the Plan included a proposal to halt the construction of the plutonium-fueled Clinch River breeder reactor. But this led to further complications. Other countries, such as West Germany and France, were concentrating on the development and world-wide sale of plutonium-fueled breeders. As an inducement to give up this program, the Plan offered them access to U.S. nuclear fuel. The currently limited U.S. capacity for the critical step in nuclear fuel production—enrichment—would be expanded, and this service would be guaranteed to "any country which agrees to comply with our nonproliferation objectives and is willing to accept certain conditions."

The expansion of nuclear fuel production was linked in turn to the Plan's proposal for a sharp increase in the current rate of nuclear power plant construction. Recognizing some of the numerous objections to such plants, however, the Plan also called for intensified inspection of nuclear plants, "firm" criteria to avoid locating them near densely populated or vulnerable natural areas, and a new review of the nuclear waste disposal program.

One of the chief reasons for the intricacy of the Plan's proposals was that they were designed to operate through a large part of the federal government's elaborate bureaucracy. The Plan used taxes as a means of manipulating energy consumption, and offered a variety of tax credits as a reward for saving energy. As a result, the Plan's provisions were deeply entwined in the operation of the Treasury Department. Many other federal agencies would also participate in the Plan's programs. The Federal Home Loan Mortgage Corporation would offer loans for energy conservation; the Labor Department would supply funds under the Comprehensive Employment and Training Act (CETA) to provide labor for the residential conservation program; the Department of Agriculture, in cooperation with the Farmers' Home Administration, would implement a rural home weatherization program; the Department of Commerce, through its local public works programs, would encourage conservation measures by state and local governments; the Department of Housing and Urban Development would introduce mandatory insulation standards; the Office of Management and Budget would see to it that energy consumption in federal buildings was reduced; the Federal Power Commission would establish new rates and procedures designed to save electricity; the Environmental Protection Agency's air pollution standards for power plants would be reviewed; the Department of the Interior would intensify coal research; the Nuclear Regulatory Commission would tighten nuclear plant inspections and the reporting of accidents and equipment failures; the Corps of Engineers would look into the potential for more hydroelectric power, especially at small sites; the Department of Transportation would develop fuel-efficiency standards for cars and trucks; all federal agencies would be directed to buy more fuel-efficient vehicles.

Despite such elaborate provisions, there was a curious omission in the administration's initial descriptions of the National Energy Plan—Mr. Carter's speeches to the nation and to Congress, and the White House *Fact Sheet.* Although the Plan's goals, and the proposed ways of achieving them, were spelled out in detail, the documents did not report what the Plan would actually accomplish. We were not told, for example, just how much energy would be saved by the elaborate conservation program and how much oil we would then avoid importing.

What was missing was a description of precisely what changes the Plan would make in the existing, very faulty, national energy budget. Yet it was evident from the administration's documents that such a projected energy budget must have been computed by the White House staff that drew up the Plan. For example, although the White House documents did not specify how much energy would be consumed in 1985 (the Plan's target date) with the Plan in effect, the *Fact Sheet* asserted that the 6 million barrels of oil that would be imported per day in that year would amount to about one-eighth of total energy consumption. Thus the total consumption figure must have been known although not stated. Nevertheless, such explicit numbers were precisely what was needed in order to judge the Plan by what it would actually accomplish rather than by what it was intended to do.

This comparison became possible when, on April 29, the White House released a 103-page book called *The National Energy Plan.* Nearly all of the volume was devoted to an elaboration of the principles, goals, and proposals already set out in the earlier documents. However, on pages 95 and 96 there was something new: tables of numbers which described what the Plan would accomplish if it was adopted. The tables were laid out in three columns. One column listed the actual amounts of different forms of energy consumed by various sectors of the economy in 1976, the latest year for which such statistics were available. The second column listed the corresponding amounts of energy that would be consumed in 1985 if the Plan was not adopted and present energy policies were continued. The third column listed the expected 1985 energy consumption figures if the Plan was adopted. A similar table showed the amounts of different forms of energy that were supplied in 1976, and the amounts that would have to be supplied in 1985 with and without the Plan. From these tables it is possible to compare what the Plan claimed to do with what it could actually be expected to do.

Such a comparison leads to some very surprising results. In many crucial places the Plan's words and numbers disagree. The disparity is particularly noticeable in the matter of energy conservation. In his speech to the nation Mr. Carter said that "the cornerstone of our policy is to reduce demand through conservation. Our emphasis on conservation is a clear difference between this plan and others, which merely encouraged crash production efforts." The same theme was emphasized in the speech to Congress, in the *Fact Sheet,* and in the text of *The National Energy Plan.* Clearly, according to the administration, the main purpose of the Plan was to meet the energy crisis by cutting demand rather than by increasing supplies; by encouraging energy conservation rather than by adding to energy production. In fact, the oil industry, which is naturally interested in selling more fuel—at a price—attacked the Plan for such undue emphasis on the demand side of the demand-supply equation.

What the Plan would in fact do to cut demand, or to increase energy supplies, can be computed by simple arithmetic from the tables published in *The National Energy Plan.* Thus, according to the tables, in 1985 total demand for energy would amount to 48.3 millions of barrels of oil per day (MBD)—without the Plan and 46.4 MBD with the Plan. So the Plan would save the difference between 48.3 and 46.4—1.9 MBD—or about 3.9 percent of the total energy demand expected in 1985.

But in a sense this is not a fair way to evaluate the impact of the Plan, since a large part of the total demand expected by 1985 was already built into the national energy system by 1977, when the Plan was proposed. It is more meaningful to judge the Plan's impact by examining, not the total demand in 1985, but the *increment* in demand that would occur while the Plan was actually in effect. This figure can be computed from the difference between the expected demand for energy in 1985 and the current demand (which is given in the *Plan*'s tables by the latest available figures, for 1976). Now the picture looks like this: Without the Plan, between 1976 and 1985 demand was expected to rise by 11.3 MBD, and with the Plan in effect, by 9.4 MBD. So the Plan's conservation measures would reduce the *increment* in demand between 1976 and 1985 by 17 percent. All the rest of the expected increase in the demand for energy between 1976 and 1985—83 percent—would be met, not by conservation, but by increasing the supply of energy. Numerically, then, the main

thrust of the Plan was to increase energy supply rather than reduce demand—just the reverse of what the administration and even its oil company critics *claimed* the Plan would do.

The tables provide some further details. Apart from conservation, about 50 percent of the added demand for energy would be met by increasing the supply of coal, 23 percent by increasing the production of nuclear power, 9 percent by increasing domestic oil production, and the rest—less than 2 percent—by solar energy. Judged by these numbers, rather than by Mr. Carter's prose, the Plan relied more on nuclear power (23 percent) than on conservation (17 percent) to meet new demand for energy. The Plan's "cornerstone" seemed to have been mislaid.

Mr. Carter also emphasized that the Plan was fair, and its fifth principle states: "Our solutions must ask equal sacrifices from every region, every class of people, every interest group. Industry will have to do its part to conserve, just as consumers will." However, the actual numbers about where the limited supplies of energy available in the 1976–85 period would go revealed a major inequity.

The degree of sacrifice made by different sectors of society depends on the equitable distribution of the available energy and the required conservation effort among them. Any sector given preferential access to available energy supplies would enjoy a distinct economic advantage; any sector required to meet a disproportionately large part of the energy conservation effort would be making an inequitable sacrifice. One of the fundamental divisions in the U.S. economy is between consuming and producing sectors. The relative amounts of energy that the Plan would make available to these two sectors can be estimated from the division of energy consumption among the three categories that are customarily included in energy statistics: residential and commercial, industrial, and transportation. The energy share allotted to consumers is roughly equivalent to that used by the residential/commercial sector. (Residential energy is, of course, used by consumers, and the energy used by commercial establishments, such as shops, is largely devoted to the sale of consumer goods, and its cost contributes to the price of such goods.) How energy supplies and conservation are shared between the residential/commercial and the industrial sectors is therefore a useful way to evaluate the equality of sacrifice of consumers and industry.

The tables published in *The National Energy Plan* provide the necessary figures. In 1976 both the residential/commercial and the industrial sectors received 37 percent of the total available energy, the rest going to transportation. However, with the Plan in effect, 74 percent of the energy added between 1976 and 1985 would go to industry and only 15 percent to the residential/commercial sector. Although the Plan would give industry a disproportionately large share of the new energy available between 1976 and 1985, both sectors would carry about the same conservation burden. Computing from *The National Energy Plan* tables, under the Plan 40 percent of the savings in energy would be accomplished in the industrial sector and 45 percent in the residential/commercial sector. Thus, although consumers would be given only one-fifth of the added energy allotted to industry (in contrast with their present, equal shares), the burden of conservation would be carried about equally by the two sectors. Despite the administration's claims of "equality of sacrifice," the Plan allotted a much larger share of the burden to consumers than to industry.

These same figures revealed a curious disparity between the expected contribution of the transportation sector to energy conservation and the elaborate effort, mandated by the Plan, to achieve it. The tables showed that conservation measures in the transportation sector would save only 3 percent of the increase in energy demand between 1976 and 1985—an achievement that hardly seemed to warrant the Plan's elaborate scheme of gas-guzzler and gasoline taxes and rebates.

In addition to these disparities between what the Plan claimed to do and what—according to the numbers published in *The National Energy Plan*—it would in fact do, the numerical data also revealed certain internal contradictions in the Plan itself. In particular, they illuminated a sharp conflict between two of the Plan's chief aims: energy conservation and increased use of coal and nuclear power. To appreciate this problem, one should recall that the efficiency with which energy is used depends greatly upon an appropriate match between the form of the energy and the particular task to which it is applied. For example, in heating a home it is far more efficient to obtain the heat directly from the combustion of a fuel (in a furnace, for example) than from an electric heater that is supplied by power gener-

ated, at the power plant, from burning fuel. One reason for the considerable waste of energy in the U.S. is that a good deal of our electric power—about 15 percent in 1974—is used, inefficiently, for space heat and hot water. A major way to conserve energy is to reduce the use of electricity for space heat and hot water.

The National Energy Plan did the reverse. It strongly altered the present balance between the use of fuel for direct heat and for electricity—in the wrong direction. In 1976, 46 percent of the total amount of energy consumed in the United States was used for direct heat and 28 percent for conversion to electricity. According to *The National Energy Plan* tables, with the Plan in effect, 36 percent of the energy added to the national budget in the period 1976–85 would be used directly for heat and 53 percent for conversion to electricity. This shift would sharply reduce the overall efficiency with which the fuel is used; it is an *anti*-conservation measure. The increased production of electricity is reflected in the Plan's heavy emphasis on the use of coal and nuclear power. All nuclear fuel and most of the coal would be used to produce electricity; these fuels would meet 74 percent of the added demand for energy in 1976–85.

Thus there were serious discrepancies between the administration's insistent, repeated claims about what the Plan would do to relieve the energy crisis and the quite opposite conclusions that emerged from the tables provided in the White House's own publication on the Plan. For some reason, either the administration's claims about the Plan, or the numbers that presumably describe its effects, were wrong.

During the weeks that followed the announcement of the Plan the White House energy staff confronted these discrepancies at several public meetings held to discuss the Plan. At a meeting of the National League of Cities on May 10, 1977, where these numerical analyses were first presented, one of Schlesinger's assistants was asked to comment on them. He was unable to respond, he said, because he was unfamiliar with the mathematical technique used to derive the figures. He seemed surprised to learn that the data were obtained simply by subtracting one column in the *Plan*'s tables from another. In June, S. David Freeman, a member of Schlesinger's staff at the time, and I debated the merits of the Plan before a meeting of the New York Bar Association. Confronted by the numerical analysis, Mr. Freeman advised me to ignore the data presented in the *Plan*'s tables. Later, in an interview with a *New York Times* reporter, he said, with reference to my analysis: "He takes those numbers and treats them as though our whole program were keyed on them. I don't think those numbers are worth talking about."

However, the numbers were not included in *The National Energy Plan* by chance; they were introduced for the explicit purpose of testing how well the Plan would do what it was supposed to do:

The first test of the Plan is whether it would make a significant improvement in the trends in energy usage that have produced the energy crisis. . . . The effects of the Plan on consumption and supply are shown in Figures IX-1 and IX-2 [these figures are the tables].

If, as Mr. Freeman asserted, the numbers are not worth talking about, then at some point in their derivation, something must have happened to destroy their significance as a measure of what the Plan would do. Given that the Plan was designed to save us from "an economic, social and political crisis that will threaten our free institutions," it seemed important to learn when and how these numbers lost their power to determine whether the Plan can achieve this urgent purpose.

2

"WONDER COOKIE": The Politics of Deceit

The National Energy Plan was a statement of government policy, intended to achieve certain national goals. Like all policies, the Plan was subjective, at best a promising intention, at worst a vain hope. But to succeed, the Plan had to take certain objective realities into account. However cleverly devised, persuasively promoted, or vigorously enforced, no government policy can, after all, change the fact that oil is a nonrenewable resource which will rise rapidly in price as dwindling reserves become harder to reach. Nor can it change the fact that it costs a great deal more to build a nuclear power plant than to drill an oil well with a comparable energy yield. Government policy can increase oil production, but that would mean higher costs per barrel. Government policy can increase the amount of energy produced per dollar invested, but that would mean favoring oil wells over nuclear power plants. Policy can change the national energy system, but only in harmony with certain objective physical and economic facts.

The authors of the National Energy Plan were well aware of these constraints. But harmonizing an energy policy with the real world which it is intended to influence is a formidable task. Energy policy is intricately involved with physical energy resources, with the elaborate system of machinery that produces, transports, and uses energy, and with the complex economic interactions that govern industrial and agricultural production, both in the United States and in the world. An energy policy must start with sound information about these interwoven affairs. And since many of them move slowly (it takes up to twelve years to build a nuclear power plant, for example), the policy must be designed to affect conditions some years ahead. Somehow the energy planner must foresee, in considerable detail, a very complex future.

According to *The National Energy Plan,* the instrument that was used to obtain a "reliable picture of America's energy future, both with and without the Plan," was something called a "mathematical model." It would be easier to find the source of the conflict between the Plan's words and its numerical forecasts if its authors had given us a glimpse into this crystal ball. Unfortunately, there is no published account of how the White House energy staff used this "mathematical model" to devise the Plan and to test its future effects on the national energy system. However, like everything the government does, the creation of the Plan has left a paper trail—memoranda and reports written for other purposes that contain bits of information from which it is possible to reconstruct how the Plan's tables of numbers were computed and how they relate to its aims.

The mathematical model on which the Plan is based is known as PIES—which stands for Project Independence Energy System. Physically, PIES is a number of reels of magnetic tape on which are recorded two types of information. One set of tapes contains the "program." This describes the expected relationships among the numerous factors that are involved in the energy system, for example: how much more oil would be found in the United States in response to a given effort to find it; what increase in the price of petroleum products would occur if federal price controls were lifted; how much energy is used relative to the size of the gross national product (GNP); how various factors, such as GNP, the world price of oil, and interest rates, are expected to change in future years. A very large number of such relationships, woven together in accordance with appropriate physical and economic concepts, comprise the "mathematical model" of the U.S. energy system. The second set of tapes contains the actual data, obtained in recent years, that are relevant to these relationships, for example: the intensity of oil exploration efforts (as given by the number of drilling rigs used) and the amount of oil found annually; the recent record of the prices of world oil and domestic petroleum products; the annual consumption of various forms of energy in recent years. When these tapes are inserted into appropriate computers, the model is made to "run"—that is, the numerical values in the second set of tapes are entered into the mathematical operations established by the first set of tapes. After the computers perform a vast number of enormously complex calculations, they print out tables of figures that predict how the energy system is expected to behave under whatever set of circumstances has been entered in the program.

The main output of the PIES model—called by its custodians, with no further explanation, "Wonder Cookie"—is a set of numerical tables that describe how the U.S. energy system is expected to look on an average day in 1980, 1985, and 1990. For each of these years, the tables forecast how much of what kinds of energy will be used by different regions of the country and by various sectors of the economy, and what they will pay for it; how much energy of different kinds the United States will produce or import, and at what cost. Usually several forecasts are made. One, called the "Base Case" (or, more irreverently, the "business as usual" case), predicts the energy situation if present policies—for example, on oil price regulation—continue into the future. Other cases, or "scenarios," predict the situations expected if new policies of various kinds are introduced. If all goes well and the different forecasts seem believable, they offer the policy-maker a choice of alternative future energy conditions, and specify the policies that will bring each of them to pass.

The Carter administration inherited PIES from the Nixon and Ford administrations. The original model was created to provide factual support for a policy that Nixon pronounced in response to the 1973 oil embargo. By then deeply embroiled in the Watergate problem, he apparently realized that the embargo represented an added political threat. Public opinion polls showed that most people blamed the federal government for the problems created when the embargo was imposed. Although the U.S. was then importing 36 percent of its oil, Nixon decided that with "discipline. self-restraint and unity," imports could be reduced to zero by 1980. On November 7, 1973, he ordered the

Federal Energy Administration (FEA) to find a way of carrying out that policy. The PIES model was created for that purpose.

The FEA experts knew that they could never make good on Nixon's promise. Fortunately for them, Nixon was forced to resign before their report was due. When Gerald Ford became President, he accepted his advisers' suggestion that Nixon's goal of zero imports by 1980 should be quietly dropped. When the *Project Independence Report*—a 781-page document accompanied by some twenty volumes of background data—was issued in November 1974, it hardly mentioned the original mandate.

Creating the PIES model was a huge, complicated task. About two thousand professional people were involved. They were recruited from twenty-three government agencies and a number of private consulting firms. Inevitably, the available accounts of PIES's birth are colored by its bureaucratic origins. One account begins in the following way:

In April [1974] the process of operationalizing the conceptual framework began. Several questions had to be answered. What was to be the planning horizon? What level of spatial aggregation would be attempted? Given the time constraints on the analysis, what was the best type of system to be used? What kind of validation procedure could the effort be subject to . . . ?

In plainer language, "planning horizon" means how far into the future the model's predictions should go (1990 was chosen). "Spatial organization" means the model's geographic scale (it is national, with regional subdivisions). "Time constraints" refers to the time in which the model had to be completed (one year). "Validation procedure" refers to ways of estimating how accurately the model would predict future events.

Two types of validation procedures were used. One dealt with the accuracy of the numerical data that were to be fed into the computer model. The series of linked commands that comprise the model are carried out by the computers blindly, so to speak, neither the accuracy of the incoming information nor the reasonableness of the resulting answers being questioned. The answers are therefore only as good as the incoming data; in computer shorthand, "garbage in, garbage out."

The remedy is careful checking of all the data entered into the tapes before they are used in the computations.

A second feature of the validation procedure deals with a more serious difficulty—faults in the internal structure of the model, in the relationships that establish the commands the computer follows in generating the answers. If a model contains such structural faults, it will yield false results whether the incoming data are good, bad, or indifferent. Suppose, for example, that one of the model's tasks is to predict the expected price of oil in 1985 from a progression of past prices. This price has been rising for a number of years, but at a much faster rate after the 1973 embargo than before. The outcome of the mathematical process that the model uses to predict the future price from the past trend—extrapolation—depends on how the computer is told to evaluate what happened in the past. If the model uses a series of pre-1973 numbers in extrapolating the trend, the price predicted for 1985 will be much smaller than it will be if post-1973 numbers are used. Which procedure is likely to yield the best prediction is a matter of judgment. If the jump in the price of oil during the embargo was only temporary, it might be better to base the prediction on the earlier numbers. If the increase was representative of a future pattern, it would be better to use the later numbers. As it has turned out, the price of oil has continued to rise since 1973, and a model based on the earlier figures would predict a 1985 price that is likely to be wrong, so that any expectations that depend on that price will also be wrong. Such an internal, structural fault can be corrected only by exposing the model-builders' original judgment to the criticism of other experts. Then the reasoning behind the decision is at least made explicit, so that it can be corrected if it contradicts current judgments or if it later turns out to be off the mark.

This kind of validation guards against one of the serious—and indeed dangerous—weaknesses of mathematical models: their internal structure, the rationale that governs their operations and determines their results, is often difficult to perceive. Because of the enormous complexity of a model such as PIES, an internal structural fault is easily hidden from all but expert eyes. And there is another, related danger. Since the computer is, after all, a *machine,* which is governed by the unequivocal rigor of mechanical or electronic

processes, its output—those long, laconically labeled, orderly tables of densely packed numbers—take on an aura of unassailable truth. There is the danger, then, that the model's hard, seemingly unambiguous output may mask its internal softness and conceal the fact that its mathematical operations are based on faulty, or at least doubtful, judgments. If a model is given faulty data, so that its output is also wrong ("garbage in, garbage out"), the difficulty is readily perceived and easily corrected. If a model's internal structure is faulty, it is likely to commit a more serious and much less noticeable error, which might be called "goodies in, garbage out." The basic defense is to ensure that the reasons for the internal design of the model are openly stated, are reviewed by outside experts, and if need be, corrected. To validate the original PIES model, FEA had its design reviewed by a series of outside committees made up of experts from universities, industry, and government agencies.

Because of the importance of the PIES model in devising government policy, such threats to its validity were particularly troublesome. Policy is designed to influence the real world, in this case the production and use of energy. But if the picture of reality that emerges from a computer model such as PIES depends, as it does, on technical judgments that the experts build into it, policy can in fact be covertly determined by the experts who make these judgments. The Nixon White House was singularly lacking in personnel with both enough technical training and sufficient loyalty to Nixon's views to serve as watchdogs over the complex inner workings of PIES. To the Nixon administration PIES seemed to be a "black box" that delivered forecasts without revealing how they were arrived at—a modern, electronic oracle. Worse than that, the model might be designed with a built-in bias that would force it to print out answers that conflicted with administration policies; the oracle might even talk like a Democrat. For these reasons Nixon's Office of Management and Budget set up its own watch over the PIES operation by asking the National Science Foundation to make an independent review specifically for OMB.

All this was rendered moot by Nixon's resignation. In the political interregnum of the Ford administration, the *Project Independence Report* was soon forgotten. On the other hand, the PIES model which produced it survived and flourished.

It was badly needed. Until Project Independence, information about the nation's energy situation came almost exclusively from the National Petroleum Council (NPC). Although nominally appointed by the Secretary of the Interior, the NPC members were chiefly oil company officials—people not known for unbiased views on energy matters. During the intense debates set off by the 1973 embargo, there were frequent complaints that depending on the NPC as a source of energy information suffered from the same defect as relying on the fox to count the chickens.

PIES gave the government a way of counting its own chickens. Congress took advantage of this opportunity, and in August 1976 passed the Energy Conservation and Production Act, which in addition to some conservation measures, mandated the establishment of a new government agency to gather and analyze energy data: the Office of Energy Information and Analysis (OEIA).

The act required that OEIA "develop a National Energy Information System containing accurate, coordinated, comparable and credible energy information . . . for energy-related policy decisions by the Federal Energy Administration (FEA), other government agencies, the Congress, the President and the public." The act describes the "National Energy Information System" in terms that establish its identity with the PIES model. As one review of the legislation has pointed out, it was enacted

> Because Congress lacked confidence in the energy data and analyses it was receiving . . . The absence of credible data and analyses has not only hampered the Congress, the President, and the executive departments from evaluating intelligently the array of energy alternatives facing the country, but also contributed to the widespread public skepticism about the seriousness of the energy crisis.

The act was also designed to guard against the danger that energy information produced by the new government agency might, like the oil companies' information, be distorted—in this case by the influence of government policy-makers. The act took the unusual step of creating an official watchdog over OEIA—the Professional Audit and Review Team (PART), composed of experts from five government agencies outside of FEA. PART was required to send Congress an annual review

of OEIA activities, including the design and use of the PIES model. Another safeguard was the provision "that OEIA be organized as a separate entity within FEA, insulated from FEA's role in formulating and advocating national policy." The act also provides that OEIA reports are to be issued without prior approval of FEA. (FEA and OEIA are now part of the new Department of Energy, but OEIA retains its independent status.)

In 1976 an improved version of the PIES model was used to produce more accurate predictions of how the U.S. energy picture was likely to develop between 1976 and 1985. These were summarized, along with the revised PIES model, in OEIA's first annual report to Congress, *The 1976 National Energy Outlook.* The model was then further refined in preparation for the 1977 annual report, which was issued on January 15, 1977, but only in draft form.

Up to this point the procedures used to develop and validate the several versions of PIES met the standards for protecting the integrity of the model and for insulating it from the influence of policy-makers. Records were kept of who made model changes and why. Outside experts reviewed the model's structure and its underlying assumptions. The 1976 version of PIES was reviewed by a number of consultants, including five major academic computer groups. There is no evidence that government policy-makers intruded on the design of the model.

Then, early in 1977, the procedures that were supposed to protect the integrity of the PIES model broke down. The draft 1977 "National Energy Outlook," published in January, was never revised or published in final form. The version of the PIES model on which this report was based was not reviewed by outside professional groups. Something had happened to disrupt seriously the normal procedures that until then had governed the management of the PIES model. What happened is clear from PART's first annual review of OEIA activities—the Carter administration came into power:

> Since the Carter Administration took office at the beginning of this year [1977], OEIA's method of operation has been to quickly provide analytical products requested by the energy policy and planning staff in the Executive Office of the President—at the expense of meeting its other responsibilities mandated

by the Congress in the Energy Conservation and Production Act. The energy policy and planning staff was responsible for developing the National Energy Plan, which the President announced on April 29, 1977, and for doing subsequent analysis in support of the plan. OEIA's credibility was harmed by becoming, in effect, an extension of the energy policy and planning staff, by failing to make public the results of all its forecasts and the assumptions upon which they were based, and by neglecting its basic responsibility to meet the needs of the public as required by law.

The PART report then makes the harsh accusation that, contrary to the purpose of the legislation that established PIES's official role in energy policy, the Carter administration violated the integrity of the model. According to the report, at the behest of the White House energy staff, the PIES model was so altered that its output supported administration energy policy:

> ... the Executive Office of the President's energy policy and planning staff, in developing the National Energy Plan, *was able to direct changes in certain economic assumptions in the PIES model* [emphasis added]. These assumptions altered not only the forecasts of energy supply and demand made for the President's energy policy and planning staff, but all subsequent forecasts as well. . . . The net impact of the 21 changes to the PIES model was to increase anticipated energy demand by the equivalent of 2.52 million barrels of oil a day by 1985 and to decrease anticipated estimated supply by the equivalent of 1.44 million barrels of oil a day by 1985. The increased gap between projected energy supply and demand translated into a greater dependence on imported oil, thus emphasizing the need to implement the President's energy plan.

Evidently the safeguards established by Congress failed to protect the integrity of the PIES model from the White House energy staff. The PART report helps to explain how that happened and how, in turn, the White House–directed changes in the PIES model led to the appearance in *The National Energy Plan* of the tables of data that conflicted so strongly with the President's

claims about the Plan. All this becomes clear from an examination of the OEIA documents that are cited in the PART report in support of their criticism of the role played by OEIA—and the White House energy staff—in the development of the National Energy Plan. From these documents it is possible to reconstruct the events that enabled the White House energy staff to alter the PIES model to their own purposes.

The events began with a conference on February 15, 1977, between George R. Hall of the White House energy staff and John D. Christie, the ranking official of the OEIA staff and the person responsible for the PIES model. One outcome of that meeting was a memorandum, dated February 17, 1977, from Christie to Hall and Alvin L. Alm, then deputy to the head of the White House energy office, James Schlesinger. The subject of the memorandum was "Base Case Specifications for the President's Program." The "Base Case" was supposed to describe the national energy picture expected in 1985 if the National Energy Plan was not enacted and present policies continued. This was to provide a base line against which the proposed effects of the Plan on the energy situation could be measured. The PIES model was to be used to establish the Base Case, by forecasting energy supply, demand, and prices in 1985, in the absence of the Plan. The expected effect of adopting the Plan on the 1985 energy situation would be determined in comparison with these Base Case predictions. Thus the expected impact of the Plan's policies depended on the nature of these predictions.

The Christie-to-Hall memorandum described a series of "important variables" that would influence the outcome of the Base Case computation. In each instance the memorandum offered two or more alternative values of the variable, usually recommending that a particular one be used in the model for the purpose of making the needed forecasts.

One week later, on February 23, 1977, a memorandum from George R. Hall of the White House staff replied to the Christie memorandum. It began:

> This memorandum responds to your memorandum of February 17 and the questions we discussed at our meeting on February 15. For analysis of the President's energy policy, we approve the use of the FEA's PIES model as

presented in Table B-3 of the draft NEO/77 (NEO/77 Reference Scenario) except for the changes noted below. ["NEO/77" is the draft 1977 "National Energy Outlook," which described the latest version of the PIES model and the outcome of various forecasts based on it.]

The main features of this dialogue by memorandum are worth recording here.

On oil price controls:

Present policy is governed by a law that establishes price controls until 1979, when they would expire if no further action is taken. The available options offered in the Christie-to-Hall memorandum were that price controls would be continued after 1979 or dropped at that time. The memorandum noted that maintaining controls, in comparison with eliminating them, would cause oil imports in 1985 to increase by 5 percent. It recommended that the model should assume that controls would be removed.

Hall replied: "Do not use the Recommended Specification. Instead assume continuation of controls indefinitely." Thus Hall's choice arranged that the model's forecast of 1985 imports would rise by 5 percent.

On the frequency of offering Outer Continental Shelf (OCS) oil and gas leases:

The government holds periodic auctions of leases to various offshore oil and gas sites, so that the frequency of such auctions determines the effort to find and produce these fuels. The Christie-to-Hall memorandum offered an option of four, five, or six auctions of leases per year, pointing out that compared with five sales per year, six sales would increase oil and natural gas production (by 300 million barrels per day and 300 billion cubic feet per year respectively) and that the four-sales-per-year option would correspondingly decrease production. Five sales per year was recommended, with six sales as an alternative.

The Hall-to-Christie memorandum replied: "OCS leasing schedule. Use neither the FEA Recommended Specification [i.e., five sales per year] nor the suggested Alternative Specification [six sales]. Instead assume that only four sales per year will be accomplished. . . ."

By overriding both of the offered alternatives,

the White House office built into the PIES model a structure that would reduce the predicted domestic supply of oil and natural gas.

On energy conservation programs:

The Christie-to-Hall memorandum states that "The specification here is of central importance in assessing the impacts of the President's program," and then provides a table, taken from the draft NEO/77 report, showing the effect on national energy consumption of conservation measures that were expected to take effect by 1985, *without* the Plan enacted.

The Hall-to-Christie memorandum replied:

Conservation Progress [*sic*]. The savings due to conservation in the NEO/77 Reference Scenario appear to us to be much too high. We would like your staff, and Scott Bush, to work with us and our consultants, Bill Stiff and Hoff Stauffer, to develop a set of numbers about which we can all feel comfortable.

Again Hall's reply follows a pattern. Apparently, the White House energy staff wished to build into the PIES model estimates of the probable future impact of existing conservation efforts that would be low enough to "feel comfortable," thus raising the expected demand for energy.

The exchange of memoranda between Hall and Christie clearly violated the integrity of the PIES model. Contrary to the intention of the Energy Conservation and Production Act, Hall, speaking for the White House energy policy office, issued instructions that seriously changed the structure of the PIES model. None of these changes were known—let alone reviewed—by outside experts, and their validity was never established.

The changes in the PIES model dictated by the White House energy office were apparently not made at random, as judged by their effect on the model's predictions. Nearly all the changes managed to *decrease* the supply of domestic energy and *increase* the demand forecast for the 1985 Base Case (that is, what was expected to happen without the enactment of the Plan). Since the gap between domestic supply and demand could be met only by oil imports, the net result of the changes ordered by the White House energy staff was to forecast considerably larger imports in 1985, in the absence of the Plan, than those predicted by the PIES model before it was altered.

This result is carefully commemorated in the next item in the National Energy Plan's paper trail—a document labeled "Memorandum for the Record," prepared by Elizabeth MacRae of OEIA on July 25, 1977. The MacRae memorandum carries the title "Differences Between the Draft NEO/77 Reference Case and the President's Program Base Case for 1985." It is an internal memorandum intended only to record for the OEIA files what changes were made in the PIES model in producing the forecasts used in the National Energy Plan, both in the model's structure and the data fed into it, and in the description of the "Base Case" scenario.

The MacRae memorandum lists twenty-one changes in the PIES model ordered by the White House energy staff and computes the effect of each on the energy supply and demand predicted for 1985. On the demand side, the net effect of the changes was to increase the forecast for 1985 given by the PIES model from 91.3 quads to 96.6 quads. (The quad is a convenient measure of the very large amounts of energy that are involved in national figures. Quad stands for quadrillion BTU [British thermal units]; it is equivalent to 180 million barrels of oil.) Thus the changes in the model ordered by the White House energy staff caused a net *increase* of 5.3 quads in the predicted demand for energy. On the supply side, the changes reduced expected total domestic energy production from 75.2 quads to 72.2 quads, a net *decrease* of 3.0 quads. Thus, according to the MacRae memorandum, in preparing the National Energy Plan, the White House staff had ordered changes in the PIES model which increased the domestic energy gap that would have to be met by imports in 1985 by a total of 8.3 quads (8.1 quads oil and 0.2 quads gas).

Before it was changed by the White House energy staff, the PIES model predicted that if present energy policies continued, oil imports would amount to 16.4 quads in 1985. Thus the changes made by the White House staff increased imports to 24.5 quads, or half again larger than they were originally. (In the tables of *The National Energy Plan,* the import figure is given as 11.5 million barrels per day [23 quads] per year, because a technical factor in the oil supply ["refinery gain"] was entered into the tables erroneously and also because of an unexplained decrease of 0.8 quads in the figure for domestic oil production.) Thus the

White House energy staff had managed to create a very sizable increase in the apparent oil import problem that the country would face if the Plan was not enacted. This is the basis for the PART report's comment on the impact of the changes in the PIES model directed by the White House energy staff: "The increased gap between projected energy supply and demand translated into a greater dependence on imported oil, thus emphasizing the need to implement the President's energy plan."

All these mathematical antics were concerned only with the 1985 Base Case—a forecast of what was expected to happen to the national energy situation if the Plan was *not* enacted and present policies were continued. However, since the Base Case was the standard against which the expected effect of the Plan was to be measured, these changes seriously affected the picture of what the administration's energy policies might accomplish. According to the tables in *The National Energy Plan,* if the administration's policies were adopted, oil imports would be 14 quads in 1985. This represented a 10.5 quad reduction from the 24.5 quads of oil that, according to the same tables, we would expect to import in 1985 if the Plan was not enacted and present policies continued. But if the model had *not* been changed, the Plan's savings in oil imports would amount to only 2.4 quads, since the original model had predicted imports of only 16.4 quads in the absence of the Plan. Thus, because of the changes in the model's Base Case ordered by the White House energy staff, the savings in 1985 oil imports that the administration's policies would be expected to bring about were increased from 2.4 quads to 10.5 quads.

This manipulation is reminiscent of bargaining in a bazaar, where a merchant might quote a $24 price on an item that he is prepared to sell for $16 or less, so that when the item is finally sold for $14, the buyer will think he has won the bargain. Had it been judged against the Base Case figures of the unaltered version of the PIES model, the National Energy Plan, like the bargain, would be seen, in truth, to accomplish only a very small saving. By arbitrarily changing the PIES model, the White House staff was able to make the import-saving effect of the Plan appear to be more than four times larger than it had been before the changes were made.

Against this background one can appreciate the

curious response of Schlesinger's aide, S. David Freeman, to the evidence that the Plan's numbers conflict with its words: "I don't think those numbers are worth talking about." Given what we now know about the origin of these numbers, one might agree that they are about as meaningful as prices quoted in a bazaar. Nevertheless, the numbers did play a decisive role in the administration's arguments for the adoption of the Plan. In presenting the Plan to the joint session of Congress, Mr. Carter defined one of its major goals as follows: "To cut imports of foreign oil to 6 million barrels a day, less than half the level it would be if we did not conserve." Thus Mr. Carter informed the Congress that in 1985, without the Plan in effect, we would import more than 12 million barrels of oil per day. This corresponds to about 24 quads per year—the import figure predicted by the PIES model only after it was altered by Mr. Carter's energy staff. Had he reported the Plan's effect on imports in comparison with the import figure predicted by the unaltered model (16.4 quads), Mr. Carter would have had much feebler support for urging a conservation campaign that was supposed to be the "moral equivalent of war."

Before it was changed, the PIES model presumably represented, with respect to the national energy picture, the best available approximation of reality. But that reality seemed to diminish the need for the conservation policy that the administration wished to urge on Congress. Confronted by this discrepancy, the White House energy staff apparently chose to alter the reality. An unkind wag might say that following their ministrations, the output of the PIES model was no longer a Wonder Cookie, but an Alice B. Toklas brownie.

However, having taken this fateful step, the White House energy staff found that by artificially intensifying the import problem, they had only created further difficulties. To begin with, the enlarged 1985 import forecast achieved by arbitrarily adding 5.3 quads to the original PIES estimate of total demand and subtracting 3.0 quads from the supply meant that in devising the Plan the planners had to squeeze 8 quads more out of the 1985 supply-demand gap than would have been necessary otherwise. If the Plan were to rely entirely on conservation to close this enlarged gap, it would need to include efforts such as the widespread replacement of private cars by mass transit and of trucks by sharply expanded railroads. However, these highly effective conservation measures would require government financial intervention—a policy contrary to Carter's economic outlook—and they are noteworthy by their absence from the Plan. Thus blocked from reducing the energy gap—which they had themselves created—by expanding the Plan's conservation measures, the White House planners were forced to include in the Plan an appreciable increase in the projected domestic *supply* of energy, over what was expected if the Plan was not enacted. According to *The National Energy Plan* tables (corrected for the error and the unexplained change in oil production noted earlier), without the Plan the 1985 energy supply would be 72.2 quads (down from the 75.2 quad figure in the unaltered version of PIES), whereas with the Plan in effect the supply would be 80 quads. Thus, because the PIES model was altered, it became necessary to include in the Plan a substantial increase in the expected domestic energy supply, bringing that figure well over the forecast originally produced by the unaltered model.

This helps to explain the curious disparity between the Carter administration's repeated claim that the Plan accentuates conservation over increased energy production, and the *fact*—which is evident in the *Plan*'s tables—that the actual emphasis is just the reverse. Despite their effort to stress the Plan's conservation measures over production, because that emphasis was achieved by changing the PIES model, the Plan actually had to call for a significant increase in domestic energy production.

Having been forced to put more domestic energy production into the Plan, the White House energy staff gave themselves yet another problem: What domestic source of energy could be expanded, beyond expected trends, enough to meet this need? Increased production of domestic oil and natural gas would violate the precept on which the administration position was based. (In his televised speech to the nation on April 18, 1977, Mr. Carter said, regarding oil and natural gas: "We cannot substantially increase our domestic production.") The Plan already envisioned a sharp increase in the current rate of nuclear power production; adding another 5.1 quads would more than double that goal, which was itself highly unrealistic, given the serious troubles in the nuclear power industry. The only option was a very sharp increase in the production of coal. The White House energy staff's memorandum added 0.2 quads of coal production to the original PIES Base Case forecast, and then another 4.9 quads were added in the Plan itself. Thus, once the PIES model was altered to increase arbitrarily the gap between demand and domestic energy production, it became necessary to make an equally arbitrary increase in the projected coal production figures.

But this maneuver only created another problem. If coal production was to be increased so much (with the Plan in effect, coal production in 1985 would be nearly twice the 1976 figure), it was necessary to find some way of *using* the added coal. But this is no simple matter. Neither transportation nor the residential/commercial sector could conceivably absorb that much more coal unless we returned to coal-burning locomotives and reinstalled coal furnaces in houses and shops. Only industry and electric power production could absorb the increased coal supply; and indeed, the *Plan*'s tables added 3.4 quads to the industrial use of coal and 2.0 quads to coal-fired electricity (as compared to the original PIES model). Here, then, is an explanation of the fact that, contrary to the Plan's principle of equity, it would give industry a disproportionate share of the energy to be added to the national supply between 1976 and 1985. Only industry and electric utilities could use the extra coal; which needed to be produced to make up for the increased gap between demand and supply; that was created by the changed forecasts produced by the PIES model, after the White House energy staff had altered it.

Thus the numerical facts upon which the Plan was supposedly based contained a mathematical fabrication—the enlarged gap between projected energy demand and domestic supply that was arbitrarily introduced into the PIES model by the White House staff. This altered figure was so intricately linked to the main features of the energy system that, once introduced, its distorting effect reverberated through the structure of the system, forcing changes in the Plan that were self-contradictory and unrealistic. As a result, the integrity of the Plan was so badly compromised that its internal rationale could no longer bear close examination—which would have been essential in any serious attempt to defend it. And so it was not defended. Instead, the numerous criticisms leveled against the Plan, including the inconsistencies between its numbers and its words, were met by the administration either by silence or by an effort to reach a compromise with those critics who seemed to hold power over its legislative fate.

This is perhaps the most damaging consequence of the flawed effort to create the National Energy Plan. The inability of the Carter administration to defend its Plan seriously hindered the political process that was required to produce meaningful national action on an issue as important and pervasive as the energy crisis. The Plan was so badly flawed that when it was introduced into Congress, it was difficult to create informed, if opposed, bodies of opinion and to debate it in a manner appropriate to the democratic resolution of so momentous a national issue.

3

THE NATIONAL ENERGY ACT:
The Politics of Defeat

When Mr. Carter introduced the National Energy Plan, he warned that the alternative to adopting it "may be a national catastrophe." His commitment to the Plan was so strong that he risked his own political fate on it, asserting that:

> It's the most important domestic issue that we will face while I'm in office. And I attribute the highest possible importance to it in my own Administration. . . . I don't know anything that is more important for me to do as President . . . than to have Congress conclude their long year's work with a successful result.

As *The New York Times* commented: "Mr. Carter has left himself little margin for failure. . . . He has staked his reputation in his first year in the White House on getting an acceptable energy program."

In the months that followed the introduction of the Plan, the public perception of it—and indeed, for largely the same reasons, of the President himself—went through a remarkable transformation. When it was introduced in April 1977, the Plan was widely regarded as a clear, forceful response to an extremely serious, long-neglected problem. Mr. Carter was perceived as the sort of thoughtful, competent leader who could carry out such an urgent and complex mission within his self-imposed one-year deadline. But when the year was over, the Plan was in a shambles and the energy problem had degenerated from a crisis into chaos. No longer was Mr. Carter seen as a forceful leader; he was seen as an uncertain one, his ideas subject to sudden, unexplained changes, his principles evaporating into compromise. His prediction that his own political future would depend on the fate of the Plan had seemed to come true. Congress not only had refused to enact the

Plan, but had mauled it so badly that any eventual legislation could hardly resemble the original. When the National Energy Act was finally passed in October 1978, during the last chaotic days of the Ninety-fifth Congress, it was widely regarded as a political caricature of the original Plan. Although the legislative history of the Plan has already been entombed under heavy layers of boredom and dismay, there is a good deal to be learned from it. The legislative history of the Plan is a useful lesson in the politics of defeat.

On Wednesday, April 20, 1977, precisely in keeping with the ninety-day deadline Mr. Carter had given his energy staff, the administration's bill to legislate the National Energy Plan was presented to Congress. Known as the National Energy Act, the bill in its original form encompassed several hundred pages of complex provisions divided into two titles, thirteen parts, fifteen subparts, and 104 sections. Since the bill contained such a wide range of provisions, it fell under the jurisdiction of five standing committees in the House of Representatives. However, House Speaker Thomas P. O'Neill managed to place the bill under the firm control of a new Ad Hoc Committee on Energy, headed by Representative Thomas L. Ashley of Ohio. If this scheme was designed to prevent the bill from becoming bogged down in debate over its numerous and often bewilderingly complex provisions, it succeeded brilliantly. Without a hitch, the bill moved through the House on a fixed timetable: On July 14 the standing committees submitted marked-up versions of the bill to the Ashley committee; on August 2 the consolidated bill, only slightly revised from the original, was submitted by the committee to the full House; on August 5, after only the four days of debate allowed by the schedule, H.R. 8444, the National Energy Act, was passed by the House with a 244 to 177 vote.

Given the gravity of the energy issue and the enormous complexity of the bill, this performance might well be considered a high point in legislative efficiency, if it were not for one defect —no one knew whether the bill could accomplish what it purported to do. As Representative John Anderson of Illinois, a legislator long concerned with the energy issue and the ranking Republican member of the Ad Hoc Committee, said when the bill reached that committee:

The biggest problem the bill faces is its inability to meet its own goals. We will be far from six million barrels of oil imports in 1985. We will be far from a 10 percent reduction in gasoline consumption. We will be far from a two percent growth in energy. We will be far from 1.1 billion tons of coal being used and we will fall short of the goals of putting insulation and solar energy in American homes.

Anderson demanded that the committee hold hearings to consider such criticism, then added that "it appears that the leadership is bent upon pushing the bill out of this body at breakneck speed. The resolution before us today demands we finish seven very complex, major pieces of legislation in less than 24 hours each." His request was refused, and when the Ad Hoc Committee submitted the bill to the House, its report merely repeated the administration's original claims about the nature of the energy crisis and what the Plan would do to solve it. The report informed the House about the "alarming FEA estimate" that in the absence of the Plan, oil imports would rise to 11.5 million barrels per day in 1985—precisely the figure (23 quads per year) produced by FEA's PIES model after the White House staff had altered it. This gave the committee a powerful reason to press for approval of the bill. But the committee—and the public—could have learned about the tainted genesis of this "alarming FEA estimate" and debated its significance if the FEA officials responsible for the PIES model had been asked to testify about how it was used in designing the Plan. They were not. The hearings were perfunctory and the only substantive debate that occurred on the House floor was about the bill's provision to continue the regulation of the price of

natural gas. Republican congressmen, agreeing with the administration's theory that prices must rise to encourage conservation, pointed out that if the price was set in an unregulated "free market," oil and gas companies would have the "incentive" to produce more gas. In reply, some Democrats pointed out that the gas industry lacks the competitive structure of a free market, since there is usually only one source of supply available to the consumer. This section of the bill, like nearly all the other parts, was passed by the House with only minor modifications.

On August 5, when the bill passed the House, it appeared that the administration had won a brilliant victory, having in less than four months persuaded the House of Representatives that almost all of the complex provisions of the Plan were sound and essential. Nevertheless, only two months later, the administration's carefully orchestrated Plan was in disarray. Senator Abraham Ribicoff of Connecticut, a senior Democrat on the Senate Finance Committee, on October 5 said in response to administration testimony about the Plan's tax provisions:

Shouldn't the President admit his energy program is in shambles? All the indications are it's just not going to fly. I think energy is the nation's No. 1 issue. Shouldn't the President and Schlesinger go back to the drawing board and come up with a new program?

In two months the bill had been largely dismembered by Senate committees, which unlike the House committees were unwilling to follow administration guidelines. Quickly the Finance Committee voted not even to consider the Crude Oil Equalization Tax, according to the administration the "centerpiece" of its conservation program. The "gas-guzzler" tax was killed, as were most of the taxes designed to persuade industry to switch from oil and natural gas to coal. Another conservation measure, federally mandated reform of utility rates, was also rejected. As a final blow to the Plan, the Senate voted, contrary to the action in the House, to deregulate the price of natural gas. This was the outcome of a three-sided battle—among Carter, oil-state senators led by Russell B. Long, and Senators James Abourezk and Howard Metzenbaum. Abourezk and Metzenbaum wanted to retain regulation and keep the price of energy down in order to protect consumers from the disastrous effects of further inflation. Both Carter and Long wanted to raise energy prices, but they differed on who should benefit. Long wanted to deregulate the price so that the extra income would go to the energy corporations, on the grounds that this would enable them to produce more oil and natural gas. Carter wanted the extra cash to go to the government, in the form of a wellhead tax. Abourezk and Metzenbaum filibustered to block Long's bill for deregulating natural gas prices, but their effort was scuttled by Vice President Mondale's heavy parliamentary hand, and the bill passed.

As a result, the House and Senate bills submitted to the Conference Committee were widely divergent. Then, as the Conference Committee struggled to reconcile the Senate's vote for deregulation with the House vote against it, Schlesinger offered a "compromise" that raised prices by *both* deregulation *and* the administration's tax. Mr. Carter then disavowed his Secretary of Energy's proposal. Soon it was Christmas and everyone went home for a month.

With the new year, consideration of the National Energy Act entered what was perhaps its most bizarre phase. Officially, the bill was in the hands of the Conference Committee, where the differences between the House and Senate versions would be debated, and if possible conciliated. Again the main area of conflict was over natural gas deregulation, and the Conference Committee wrangled for weeks, and then months, over the issue. But the debate did not resolve the issue, and worse, it failed to cast much light on it. The chief reason why so little was learned from the controversy was that it largely occurred in secret. For weeks the Conference Committee simply did not meet. Instead, under the leadership of Senator Henry Jackson, those committee members who were considered sufficiently "reasonable" to work out a compromise were invited to meet privately. Together with Dr. Schlesinger, this rump group met at frequent intervals, unannounced, in the little-known rooms that abound in the niches of the Capitol's complex architecture. Finally, on April 21, Senator Jackson announced triumphantly that the secret sessions had produced a new "compromise" on gas deregulation. The members of the rump group would provide enough votes to carry the measure through the official Conference Committee when it met. This was to occur after "a few weeks," the time needed to put the agreement into legislative language. Again weeks passed with no official action. Finally, in August several key members of the rump group declared that they were dissatisfied with the agreement, and it was generally agreed that no bill would reach the floor of the Senate and the House before the preelection adjournment.

This placed the Carter administration in a serious political situation. For months Mr. Carter's standing in public opinion polls had been falling. The public dissatisfaction with the President was largely based on his inability to carry out his program, especially in energy. Some sort of energy bill was needed to overcome this view. Accordingly, the administration made a strenuous effort to find enough votes among the members of the Conference Committee to ensure that it would report out a natural gas deregulation bill. Following intensive horse-trading (Senator James McClure of Idaho was assured that a nuclear breeder would be built in his state and Representative Charles Rangel of New York received support for a hoped-for trade center), the administration rounded up the minimum of thirteen signatures needed to report out the bill. By the end of September the "compromise" deregulation bill had passed the Senate.

The final version of the National Energy Act came to a vote in the turmoil of the Ninety-fifth Congress's closing days. In the Senate, the redoubtable Senator Abourezk attempted, through a filibuster, to delay consideration of the compromise deregulation bill beyond the fixed date of adjournment, which would have killed the bill, and with it the act. He failed, and with the Senate clock stopped, in an all-night session on Saturday, October 14, the bill was passed, together with three additional bills constituting the remnants of the Plan. In the House, the administration strategy was to allow a vote only on the entire package of energy bills, so that the numerous opponents of deregulation would be forced to choose between adhering to their position and having any energy bill at all. By a one-vote margin the House Rules Committee decided to submit the single package, which in a tumultuous all-night session survived a crucial procedural vote 207 to 206, and then passed in the early morning hours.

The National Energy Act, according to the *Wall Street Journal,* bore "only a faint resemblance to President Carter's original proposals . . . there is little consensus as to what it actually will achieve." Most of the tax measures that were designed to encourage conservation by raising the cost of energy were gone, and the "gas-guzzler" tax was much weakened. Utilities were given until 1990 to switch from burning oil and natural gas to burning coal. Whereas the administration's stick and carrot approach would have penalized industries that failed to switch to coal and awarded tax credits for those that did switch, the act eliminated the stick and much reduced the size of the carrot. Tax credits designed to encourage householders to install insulation and solar devices were retained, but at lower levels than the original. Although the administration claimed the act as a victory, neither its supporters nor its opponents were happy. Representative Harley Staggers of West Virginia, who helped push the bill through the Conference Committee, said, "This is the best thing we could come up with." Representative Toby Moffett of Connecticut, who fought hard against the gas deregulation measure, said that the act would "put the cost on the back of the American consumer and won't produce the supplies we need." The cartoonist Herblock commemorated the event with a drawing depicting Mr. Carter standing in his legislative "trophy room," beaming at the skeleton of a very large fish, labeled "Energy Bill."

Some thoughtful legislators were concerned that the National Energy Act—devised under the influence of the grossest sort of political expediency and, in its final form, written in the confusion of all-night sessions—might inadvertently include some serious errors. A few months later it was apparent that their fears were justified, as it became evident that the act's provisions for higher energy prices were intensifying the country's major problem—a devastating rate of inflation. In particular, natural gas deregulation promises to have a particularly heavy inflationary impact, and it is useful to look into the pivotal role that it played in the legislative history of the act.

The price of natural gas sold in interstate commerce had been under federal control since June 1938. This was based on the reasonable notion that when residential communities and industries install gas-burning equipment, they become totally dependent on a single supplier of that fuel and need to be protected from the arbitrary price increases that are likely to be imposed by an uncontrolled monopoly. Mr. Carter's position on the issue was ambiguous, to say the least. In October

1976, in a letter to Governor Dolph Briscoe of Texas, he said that if elected, he "would work with the Congress as the Ford Administration has been unable to do, to deregulate new natural gas." Despite this promise, the original National Energy Plan provided for continued regulation of natural gas, and during the House debate on the act, with administration encouragement, Democratic representatives successfully fought off the Republican effort for deregulation. Nevertheless, in a question and answer session with the National Newspaper Association in Houston, Texas, in October 1977, Mr. Carter said: "we are working toward deregulation of natural gas." Representative Ashley, who had worked hard to enforce the administration's opposition to deregulation in the House, and faced a battle over the issue in the Conference Committee, found this remark "not helpful." In the end, the administration, over the strenuous objections of liberal Democrats in both houses, agreed to a "compromise" natural gas deregulation bill that went a long way toward providing the higher prices that the producers demanded as an incentive to look for and produce natural gas.

The bill, as it was incorporated into the final version of the National Energy Act, established a fixed schedule of yearly increases in price, ending in 1985, when all controls would be removed. This provision is likely to generate precisely the difficulties that, according to the administration, the bill was supposed to prevent—gas shortages and windfall profits. The bill will allow gas producers to calculate quite precisely the increment in price that they will be allowed for gas brought into the market at a particular date. It takes little imagination or detailed economic analysis to realize that it will pay the gas producers to drill now and sell later. In other words, the bill will encourage gas companies to hold back the sale of newly discovered gas as long as they can, in order to take advantage of the next round of price rises. This strategic response to the new bill is likely to produce short supplies of gas for the consumer and windfall profits for the producer.

These problems arise because, by establishing a set sequence of allowable prices, the natural gas deregulation bill in effect *guarantees* a particular rate of increase in the price of this crucial fuel. An even more ominous fault arises from the way in which the price sequence is set: the price of natural gas is allowed to rise at an annual rate that is 4 percent above the general rate of inflation. Thus if in 1979 the consumer price index increases, as seems quite likely, at a rate of nearly 10 percent, the price of natural gas can be increased by 14 percent. But it must be remembered that the cost of energy contributes to the cost of producing all goods and services, and therefore to their price. In this way the bill sets up a mutual self-propagating interaction between the price of energy and the general rate of inflation. The conventional view is that this is not a serious situation, because energy costs represent so small a part (about 4 percent) of average production costs that they will affect the selling price of most goods rather little. On this basis it would be expected that when the general rate of inflation is 10 percent, and the price of energy rises by 14 percent annually, it would add about 0.5 percent to the overall inflation rate.

However, this approach overlooks an important economic characteristic of energy: that unlike most other factors of production (for example, a raw material such as rubber), it is *also* an important cost to consumers, and therefore to workers. Moreover, energy represents a considerably larger fraction of the workers' living costs than of the entrepreneurs' production costs. Therefore, as the price of energy rises it will appreciably increase the workers' cost of living. In turn, this means that workers hoping to compensate for inflation will need to seek a wage increase that reflects this impact of rising energy prices on their cost of living. And since wages represent a very large part of production costs (about 75 percent, on the average), these wage demands will have a correspondingly intense effect on the prices of goods. These relationships, then, set up a cycle of economic interactions which considerably magnifies the potential inflationary impact of a rise in the price of energy. Although the direct effect of a 14 percent per year increase in the price of energy will add only 0.5 percent to the rate of general inflation, its indirect effect (on the wage increase needed to compensate for the impact of the rising price of energy on the cost of living) might well add 2.5 to 3.0 percent to the general rate of inflation. Thus, if the nation's working people were, in fact, able to obtain the wage increases needed to counteract such higher energy costs, inflation might jump from a rate of 10 percent to 13 percent.

The decision by the Organization of Petroleum Exporting Countries (OPEC) in December 1978 to increase the price of oil by 14.5 percent over the following year is another aspect of this sort of multiplier effect. As the price of energy increased in the United States, and intensified inflation, pressure on the value of the dollar in foreign markets mounted and the value declined. Since OPEC prices are quoted in dollars, this considerably reduced the effective returns on the sale of the oil, thus giving OPEC a reason to increase the price of oil—which will add to U.S. inflation and the pressure on the dollar. Once more—this time through the agency of the economy of the OPEC countries —there is a mutual interaction between the rising price of energy and general inflation which feeds on itself, magnifying the inflationary impact of higher energy prices.

In mandating higher energy prices, the Congress, and the administration, seem to have allowed a virulently inflationary genie out of the bottle, with effects that were totally ignored, let alone unanticipated, in the debate over the energy plan. The distressing lack of attention to the connection between energy and inflation was evident as late as August 1978, when Mr. Carter made the following responses in the same interview: On the "No. 1 domestic problem," he said: "Inflation has become increasingly serious now . . . we are considering a number of options to improve our anti-inflation campaign." On energy, he said: "I do believe it's necessary to see the cost of oil sold in this country go up to the world market price." That neither the President nor the several editors of a national news magazine who interviewed him found it necessary to explain, or even to take note of, the contradiction between these two statements symbolized the state of public discourse after fifteen months of futile wrangling on how to conduct Carter's "moral equivalent of war."

However, six months later, the fundamental connection between energy prices and inflation was impossible to ignore. Responding to the expected inflationary impact of the 14.5 percent increase in the OPEC oil price, the New York Stock Exchange experienced one of its worst declines of the year and the dollar resumed its plunge in foreign markets. Several months too late, the issue that should have been intensely debated in response to the administration's effort to deal with the energy crisis was suddenly brought to public attention. But the inflationary genie was by then at large and the nation was already confronted with a poorly understood but ominous economic future. This may be the price the country will pay for the political sin of attempting to deal with an issue as deep and pervasive as energy as though it were just another counter in the game of political expediency.

4

THE ECONOMICS OF ENERGY:
The Politics of Inflation

The campaign to enact the National Energy Plan began with a short-lived effort to stir up grassroots support, using television spots by John Denver and other luminaries, and local "town hall" meetings. Like the Plan itself, the campaign was conducted under the banner of conservation. The administration tried to persuade people that energy conservation was an overriding issue and that special interests and partisanship must bow to it. Some people, but not many, were persuaded. Henry Kissinger—at liberty since the Carter victory—although not known for his interest in energy while he served in the Nixon administration, became one of the leaders of a Citizens' Alliance to Save Energy. The conservation campaign also received considerable editorial support from newspapers. However, despite the Commander in Chief's declaration of the moral equivalent of war, most people refused to follow him into battle. Public opinion polls showed that many Americans did not really believe there was an energy crisis, as Mr. Carter defined it. Several times the President complained that the public "has not responded well" to his appeals.

Although Mr. Carter had placed the energy crisis first on his own list of national problems, the public's list was different. According to a Gallup poll taken in April 1977, the energy crisis was third in a ranking of important problems, behind the high cost of living and unemployment. Even after the administration's strenuous campaign to drum up interest in the National Energy Plan, a July Gallup report stated that only 15 percent of those polled believed the energy crisis to be the biggest problem the nation faced. On at least two occasions Mr. Carter had himself heard this message. When, on March 17, 1977, he attended a Charleston, West Virginia, "Energy Round Table," one of several designed to explain to the public the administration's concern with energy, Mr. Carter heard Carole Ferrell, an administrative officer with the state Human Rights Commission, say:

I sat down last night with my husband and we paid our monthly bills and I totaled up the utility bills and they came to $120. And the weather has been nice. But it is still too high. When I think about people whose welfare checks only come to $200 a month and they have to buy food stamps with that money, the cost [of energy] cannot be passed on to the consumers. There is not much more we can stand.

Later, in a similar "question and answer" session held in Detroit in October, Lawrence Hall, an unemployed steelworker, told Mr. Carter:

I am in a desperate situation now. I need a job. . . . I don't feel much like talking about energy and foreign policy. I am concerned about how I am going to live.

The gap between what was on Mr. Carter's mind and what was on his questioners' goes to the heart of the energy problem. Like the President and the unemployed worker, the administration and the American people were talking past each other, the one concerned with the abstract, distant threat of an energy shortage, the other with real, immediate problems: unemployment and inflation. According to the conventional view of politics, this was to be expected, since energy and the economy are regarded as separate issues which must compete in the political arena for attention and remedial action. Mr. Carter shared this view, for as he later admitted: "When I presented my comprehensive energy plan to the Congress in

April of 1977, inflation, although important, was not the preeminent issue in my mind." But the issues are, in fact, inseparable. Indeed, the energy crisis is basically an *economic* issue, which must be solved in order to relieve economic problems such as inflation. There is no need to await a predicted energy shortage for evidence that the crisis is real; it arrives in convincing reality with each month's utility bill. The crisis is not so much the future lack of energy as the present lack of jobs. It is impossible to understand the energy crisis without inquiring into the connection between the nature of our present sources of energy and the economic consequences of relying on them.

The basic reason for the energy crisis is that the energy sources on which we rely—oil, natural gas, coal, and uranium—are nonrenewable. These fuels were laid down only once during the earth's history, in deposits that, however large they eventually turn out to be, are surely limited in total amount. As they are used, they do indeed "run out." But we have been running out of oil ever since the first barrel was taken out of the ground in 1859. Lincoln could have declared that "we are running out of oil" as truthfully as Carter can declare it. What is not only true but relevant is that with each barrel of oil taken out of the ground, the next barrel becomes progressively more expensive. Inevitably, as a nonrenewable energy source is depleted, the cost of producing it —and therefore its price—rises faster and faster as more is produced. It is this economic feature of nonrenewable resources such as oil that causes a crescendo of trouble and mounts to a crisis. The remarkable if melancholy fact is that this crucial truth is discussed nowhere in the administration's fearsome exhortations about "running out" of oil and other nonrenewable sources of energy.

A good deal is known about the relation between the amount of fuel produced and the cost of producing it. The recent trend in the costs of producing domestic fuels in the U.S. was first analyzed in a 1972 National Petroleum Council (NPC) study, which has since been refined in several FEA reports. The results are quite consistent and clear-cut. They show that even allowing for general inflation, the cost of producing oil, natural gas, and uranium, and therefore their prices, increase at a progressively faster rate as more of these resources are produced. In this respect these nonrenewable resources are unlike manufactured goods, which ordinarily decrease in price as more are produced. Thus, according to the NPC study, in order to achieve only an 18 percent increase in the annual production of domestic oil between 1970 and 1985, the selling price of the oil (in constant 1970 dollars), based on the expected production costs and a fixed rate of profit, would need to rise from $3.18 per barrel in 1970 to $3.70 in 1975, $5.16 in 1980, and $7.21 in 1985. If a graph of these data was drawn, with the cumulative amount of fuel produced plotted on the horizontal axis and the price per barrel on the vertical axis, the line would curve upward at an ever steeper angle. By mathematically extending the course of such a curve (extrapolation), one can predict the future price of the fuel. From the above data, again discounting the effect of general inflation, it would appear that if the trend continued, domestic oil would cost $14 per barrel in 1995, $70 in 2020, $380 in 2045, and $2,000 in 2070. These numbers suggest that such a simplistic long-term extension from present trends is likely to predict only an absurdity. For example, an extrapolation based on the annual sale of black-and-white television sets in the U.S. between 1947 and 1957 predicts that the country would be literally knee-deep in television sets in 2000. Obviously, no such progression can continue indefinitely; to appreciate what it means, one needs to know how long it will last. And to understand how long a present trend will go on, one needs to learn *why* it has developed. In the case of oil and other nonrenewable fuels, the question is how their patterns of occurrence and production account for the present escalating rise in price and how long these circumstances are likely to govern the trend.

The general, mathematical nature of exponential processes is, of course, well known. The most familiar example takes place in a bank—the growth of a savings deposit at compound interest. The sum of $100 deposited at 6 percent interest will earn $6 in the first year; in the second year, with the deposit increased to $106, it will earn $6.36, and so on. As long as the process continues, the sum grows geometrically, leading to the dramatic, if usually unrealizable consequence, that after 100 years the principal will amount to about $34,000, and earn an annual interest of $2,040.

The reason for the dramatic growth of a sum held at compound interest is that there is a repeated, cyclical interaction between the two elements of the system: the size of the deposit (the principal) and the granting of interest. A series of ongoing actions takes place: The granting of interest increases the size of the principal; the enlarged principal then increases the amount of interest granted; and so on. Mathematically, these actions represent a series of multiplications, the number of which can be expressed by an *exponent*. Thus 2^3 means that the number 2 enters into the multiplication process three times ($2 \times 2 \times 2$), which amounts to 8; here the exponent is three. A relationship that is governed by such sequential multiplicative events is called *exponential*.

To appreciate why there is a similar mathematical relationship between the cost of producing a unit amount of a nonrenewable fuel such as oil and the cumulative amount produced, we need to identify the interactive process that governs the relationship. The practical situation is this: Lying at various depths beneath the surface of the United States and the surrounding waters are a limited number of fields of oil, which vary considerably in the amount and accessibility of the recoverable oil they contain. Year by year, fields are looked for, found, and then gradually drained of their oil. Why should the effort required to produce a barrel of oil—or its cost—rise *exponentially* as more and more oil is taken from the ground?

It is helpful to think about this problem on a scale that is more accessible to personal experience. Imagine a wooded grove a few days after an autumn rain, which has produced a bountiful crop of mushrooms. A nearby farmer plans to harvest the crop and sell the mushrooms at a price that covers the cost of harvesting and provides a margin of profit. Since no further rain is expected, and all the mushrooms that the grove is likely to produce have grown up at the same time, the total crop is limited in its size. At least for the present, it is a nonrenewable resource. Also, like most things that grow in the wild, the mushrooms vary considerably in their size and accessibility and therefore in the effort needed to find them, and in the cost of gathering them. Thus, this specific crop of mushrooms shares two basic attributes with the nation's oil deposits—it is a nonrenewable resource and its individual units vary in the effort needed to acquire them.

Now the harvesting begins. The farmer is anxious to gather the most attractive mushrooms at the lowest possible cost, so that they can be sold at a favorable price. Hence, on the first day of harvest he is likely to gather the biggest, best, and most accessible mushrooms. On the next day, he will search the same ground once more, but now the most desirable, easily seen mushrooms are gone, and since no new ones appear, the farmer must content himself with smaller and less accessible specimens. He will therefore be forced to do more work looking for mushrooms than yesterday, per pound of mushrooms collected. The next time around, the harvest will be even less rewarding, the earlier forays having already depleted the supply of the best and second-best mushrooms. And so on. The farmer will find that each day the difficulty of gathering mushrooms, and hence their cost, will rise at an ever-increasing rate. The cost of gathering a pound of mushrooms will increase exponentially with the total amount of mushrooms harvested.

The basic reason for this outcome is that there is a strong interaction between the gathering of mushrooms and the composition of the standing crop from which the next mushrooms are gathered. The current composition of the crop—specifically, the proportion of desirable, accessible mushrooms in it—determines the effort, or cost, of gathering them. In turn, the act of gathering mushrooms changes the composition of the crop. Each step acts on the other. When mushrooms are gathered, the proportion of the more desirable specimens in the crop is reduced; and thus altered, the new composition of the crop makes the next gathering of mushrooms more costly. As the crop is depleted, and the total amount of mushrooms gathered increases, the cost of gathering another pound of them rises in a multiplicative progression, exponentially. Finally, gathering more mushrooms will become extraordinarily costly and no further effort will be warranted. In a practical, economic sense, the grove will have then "run out" of mushrooms, although in an abstract, physical sense, a few inaccessible mushrooms will still remain.

In order to demonstrate that this relationship depends on *both* the limited size of the crop (nonrenewability) and the variable effort of harvesting individual units, we might think about what happens when the farmer harvests a field of corn. Unlike the wild crop of mushrooms, corn is cultivated, and the individual plants are essentially alike. (In a well-ordered midwestern cornfield, for example, each plant is likely to carry just one standard-size ear.) When the farmer harvests the corn, starting, let us say, with the rows nearest the storage bins, the effort required per plant will increase as the harvest progresses and rows that are increasingly distant from the bins are taken. But in this case, because the individual plants are uniform, the act of harvesting them does not change the overall composition of the crop. The standing crop becomes smaller as it is harvested, but it still consists of the same, uniformly one-eared plants. The two elements in the system—the act of harvesting and the composition of the crop—do not act upon each other. In the absence of a multiplicative interaction, the increase in effort, per corn plant harvested, is only additive and rises in direct proportion to the total amount harvested rather than exponentially.

These agricultural analogies tell us that two conditions must coexist in a harvesting or production process if there is to be an exponential relationship between the amount harvested or produced and the cost per unit. First, the system must be nonrenewable (thus, the size of the corn or mushroom crop is fixed). Second, the individual units that make up the overall system must vary in their accessibility and therefore in the cost of acquiring them (as do the mushrooms, but not the corn plants). Where both conditions exist (as well as the aim of keeping production costs as low as possible), there is the interactive, feedback relationship that characterizes an exponential process. This happens in harvesting mushrooms but not corn.

Producing oil is like harvesting mushrooms: there is a strong interaction between the act of finding and producing oil and the structure of the "crop" of accessible oil fields that remain to be found. When exploitation of the U.S. oil resource began in earnest at the turn of the century, the largest, best-yielding, most accessible fields were the first ones brought into production. The exploration and production costs were extremely low—only a few cents per barrel. But as oil was produced from the initial, large fields, the composition of the remaining oil deposits changed. Soon the big, easily exploited fields were exhausted and it became more costly to find and exploit the next-best ones. At first, when the costs were reckoned in pennies per barrel, their gradual rise was hardly noticeable. But now, after nearly one hundred years of exploitation, the cost per barrel is reckoned in dollars, and soon in tens of dollars, and the annual increase in cost is correspondingly large. Like the rate of growth of a hundred-year-old bank deposit, the rate of growth of oil production costs in the United States has become spectacularly fast.

Here, then, is the real meaning of the nonrenewability of an energy resource. The problem is not that it will become totally depleted, but that it will become too costly to produce. We will exhaust not our oil but our ability to pay for acquiring it. As in a thoroughly harvested crop of mushrooms, some oil will always remain in the ground when it becomes too costly to bring it to the surface.

However, exponential growth in the cost of producing oil or any other nonrenewable resource will persist only as long as the processes that cause the interactive relationship also continue. What usually ends the exponential rise in the cost of a particular resource is that it is replaced by a less costly substitute. That is what happened, for example, when the United States depleted a once important resource—the vast herds of buffalo in the Great Plains. In this case, the expected escalation in price certainly occurred; between 1872 and 1882, when the great buffalo herds were wiped out and the remaining animals became increasingly difficult to find, the cost of buffalo robes rose exponentially. But at a certain point they priced themselves out of the market and other goods took their place. Although as a species buffalo are of course an irreplaceable resource, viewed as a source of food and clothing they are replaceable. The exponentially more costly process of killing them was brought to a halt simply by substituting less costly sources of food and apparel, incidentally saving the species from extinction.

However, energy is different: there is no substitute for it. Whether provided by fuel-fed machines, by beasts of burden, or by people, work must be done in every production process, and work is generated *only* by the flow of energy. There is no way to avoid this thermodynamic imperative. The labor of people or animals can substitute for inanimate forms of energy, but only for certain production processes. (Thus the possibility of ever flying from New York to Rome in a vehicle powered by human or animal labor is essentially zero.) Practically speaking, then, unless we are willing to forgo most of the advantages of modern industrial and agricultural production and transportation, we must use some nonliving sources of energy. Unlike the buffalo, such sources of energy cannot be replaced in the economy as their prices escalate. And as long as we continue to depend on nonrenewable forms of energy, the interactive process that exponentially increases their price will persist. As long as we continue to use them, oil and the other nonrenewable fuels on which we depend will continue to rise in price, exponentially.

But this conclusion flies in the face of conventional wisdom, which blames the rapid rise in energy prices on the Arab nations (or, alternatively, on Israel for opposing them)—problems that, one would hope, are not likely to continue indefinitely into the future. The usual explanation for the rising price of oil is that, angered by U.S. and European support of Israel in the war with Egypt and Syria in October 1973, OPEC, led by the Arab nations, cut back oil production, inducing a world-wide shortage that enabled the cartel to raise the price from $3.01 per barrel in the summer of 1973 to $11.65 on January 1, 1974.

But the facts are quite different. To begin with, as pointed out by John M. Blair in his detailed study, *The Control of Oil:*

> In reality, the embargo occasioned only limited and temporary dislocations . . . there was no shortage of OPEC production in 1973. Indeed, in the period of the embargo—the fourth quarter of 1973—OPEC output turned out to be virtually the same as in the corresponding quarter of the following year, by which time the concern of OPEC (and the majors) had shifted to a potential surplus.

Furthermore, the real cause of the increased oil price is in the United States, not in the Arab nations. In 1973 the Arab oil ministers were well aware that OPEC's largest customer, the U.S. oil companies, had announced in the NPC report published a year earlier that the price of U.S. oil, although essentially constant (in uninflated dollars) for twenty-five years, would need to begin rising along the exponential curve. The OPEC oil ministers' response followed the normal business practice—which many of them, like their U.S. colleagues, had presumably learned at the Harvard Business School—that goods ought to be priced at what the market will bear. Clearly, if, according

to the companies that produce it, the price of domestic U.S. oil was going to escalate, it made sense for OPEC prices to do the same. The Arab-Israeli war in October 1973 only provided a convenient excuse. To help matters along, in 1974 the U.S. oil companies also raised their "target" rates of profit, and profits, which averaged 11 percent in 1963–72, increased to 19 percent in that year. The actual price of U.S. oil has neatly matched these predicted prices. For 1978 the NPC report published six years earlier had projected an average domestic oil price, in current dollars, of $7.90 per barrel (at a 20 percent rate of profit), and in June 1978 the actual price was $9.05. It would seem that well in advance of the embargo, the U.S. oil companies were able to predict—or perhaps determine—how fast the price of domestic oil would rise. Thus, contrary to conventional wisdom, the escalating price of energy, which is the only real evidence of an energy crisis, originates not with the greed or hostility of Arab sheiks, but with a more fundamental force—the inevitable economic impact of the depletion of oil in the United States (abetted, to be sure, by the oil companies' deliberate increase in their targeted rate of profit).

Because energy is used in producing all goods and services, when its price rises, the cost of everything else is driven upward. When the price of energy began to escalate in 1973, wholesale commodity prices soon followed. Before 1973, commodity prices had been inflating at a modest rate of about 2 percent a year; after 1973 they took off, going into double-digit figures in 1974, and since then running at more than 10 percent a year. And consumer prices have not been far behind. The rising price of energy has become a driving force behind the rapid rate of inflation, which is now regarded as the most serious problem facing the United States. As the *Wall Street Journal* pointed out in April 1977, when it was still possible to be somewhat light-hearted about the inflation problem:

> It's spring, a time for raising things—including prices. . . . There are more important factors than the season, of course. The most important are strengthening demand for many industrial products as the economy quickens, and a continued rise in production costs, particularly for energy and petroleum-derived feedstocks.

Inflation is a notorious evil; it reduces purchasing power, lowers the demand for goods, depresses production, and so leads to unemployment. Efforts to correct it are likely to cause an economic recession. But when inflation is driven by the rising price of energy, this bad situation becomes much worse. The prices of goods that are particularly dependent on energy are hit hardest by the rising price of energy. Unfortunately, these energy-intensive goods include housing (which depends on the cost of fuel and electricity), clothing (most of which is now made from petroleum-based synthetic fabrics), and food (which now heavily depends on fertilizers and pesticides, chemicals made out of petroleum and natural gas). This puts a particularly heavy burden on poor families, which use a much larger part of their budget to buy such necessary, energy-intensive items, as compared with wealthier families. According to an analysis of 1975 consumer expenditures, the poorest U.S. households (with annual incomes less than $1,800) spent more than 25 percent of their income on energy purchases, while the wealthiest U.S. families (with incomes of $27,000) spent only 6 percent of their income in that way. If the price of energy increases by only a third beyond present levels—a rise much smaller than that expected in the next five years—the living standards of the poorest group of families will be reduced by nearly 9 percent. When energy prices increase, everyone's living standards decline, but the poor suffer most.

The rising price of energy also has a particularly bad effect on the economy because it tends to hamper new industrial investments. When an entrepreneur invests in a new factory he needs to predict reliably the long-term cost of the necessary production factors, including energy. This is how the rate of return on the investment is computed—the famous "bottom line" that determines whether or not an investment will be made. Since 1973 the price of energy has been rising at a rate unprecedented in the history of the country. Between 1964 and 1973 the price of energy increased at an average rate of 3.7 percent per year; between 1973 and 1977 it increased at an average rate of 22.5 percent per year. For the entrepreneur the problem is not only the actual high cost of energy, which in most cases he can pass along (and sometimes a little more) to the consumer. What the entrepreneur cannot readily cope with is the high *rate of increase* in energy costs, for this sharply increases the uncertainty of future prices. Between 1950 and 1970, when energy prices were stable, the entrepreneur, in predicting the operating costs of a new enterprise, could count on an accurate forecast of future energy prices. Now that energy prices are rising so rapidly, future prices can be very uncertain, and the risk is larger that a new investment that depends on them may fail. Such uncertainties contribute to the present slow rate of investment—which means that plants are not built, and job opportunities are lost.

Another link between energy and the economy is provided by *capital,* which plays a major role in the economy and is, after all, the basic prerequisite for creating new productive activities. There have been frequent complaints from the business community that the present weakness of the economy is in good part due to the lag in new capital investment. This is an ominous sign, for a slow rate of investment in new productive enterprises today means a much lower rate of growth in productive capacity—and job opportunities—tomorrow. The availability of capital, and the willingness of investors to risk it in new productive enterprises, are essential to the economy's health.

There is a close connection between the flow of energy and capital. Energy production is extraordinarily capital-intensive—that is, relative to the economic value of its output, energy production demands much more capital than other productive enterprises. Thus, according to a recent analysis, whereas the energy industry used 15 percent of the capital available for all business investments in 1972–74, in 1975–82 it is expected to use 25 percent. As a result, the energy industry is particularly vulnerable whenever it becomes difficult to raise investment capital. This situation has often arisen in recent years, causing the abandonment or delay of energy projects that are especially capital-intensive, such as nuclear power plants and synthetic oil and shale oil projects.

The opposite connection is also important: the ways in which we now produce and use energy strongly influence the general availability of capital, and therefore the rate of new investment which depends on it. This is another consequence of the exponential relationship that governs the exploitation of a nonrenewable resource such as oil. As the resource is exploited, and the oil fields that remain become progressively deeper, smaller, and less accessible, more and larger drilling equipment and well installations are needed. This means a larger investment of capital per unit of oil produced. According to a recent study by Bankers Trust Company, even with a projected 10 percent decrease in annual production from 1976 to 1982, domestic capital requirements for the oil and natural gas industry in the United States are expected to *increase* by 23 percent (in 1976 dollars). This confirms an earlier FEA study which predicted that the productivity of capital investment in domestic oil production (that is, the amount of oil produced per dollar invested) would fall by 70 percent by 1988.

Various ways of producing energy differ considerably in their capital productivity. The most recent analysis of this problem by the American Gas Association shows, for example, that to deliver one additional quadrillion BTU (one quad) of energy per year to residential/commercial users, an electric power plant system would require an investment which is about twice that required for systems based on natural gas. For industrial use there is a three to one disparity between the capital required by the two types of energy systems. In industry, the use of coal is considerably more capital-intensive than the use of oil or natural gas. The production of synthetic oil from coal, or shale oil, is also particularly capital-intensive.

In sum, all of the harmful consequences of the nonrenewability of the energy sources on which we now depend are economic. The progressive depletion of the supplies of these energy sources results in an exponential rise in the cost of producing them, and therefore in their price. In turn, the rising price of energy intensifies inflation; it reduces the standard of living, but of the poor more than others; it hinders new industrial investments and aggravates unemployment; it intensifies the shortage of capital. The end result is a serious threat of economic depression. An energy policy that relies on higher energy prices to govern its use, that emphasizes particularly capital-intensive ways of producing energy, such as coal (as compared with oil or natural gas) and electricity, particularly from nuclear power plants (as compared with the direct burning of oil and natural gas), will intensify these economic problems.

The National Energy Plan proposed just such a policy. The Plan was deliberately designed to raise domestic energy prices to match the high-est-priced source—the world price of oil—and then to keep them pegged to that price, as it continues to rise. The Plan proposed to counteract the regressive effect of higher energy prices on the poor by means of a system of rebates that would return the extra cost to consumers. However, no such maneuver can obscure the fact that sharply rising energy prices would spread through the economy and aggravate inflation. Undiminished by rebates, the inflated prices of life's necessities would still burden the poor; the uncertainty of future energy prices would hinder investments, and industry would be less capable of creating new job opportunities; young people who might fill such new jobs—20 to 40 percent of them now unemployed—would be disappointed in that hope.

The Plan also placed a heavy and unproductive drain on available capital. It mandated a sharp shift from those forms of energy that are least demanding of capital—oil and natural gas—to those that are most demanding: coal production and the generation of electricity, especially by nuclear power plants. The Plan also required factories to convert from burning oil and gas to burning coal for industrial processes. The Plan estimated that this shift alone would consume at least $45 billion—a huge investment yielding no economic returns to the industries and preventing them from making more productive investments. At the same time, by increasing the availability of electricity (relative to direct use of fuel), the Plan would encourage those industries that are power-intensive—and are therefore likely to use electric power to replace people, thus intensifying technological unemployment. In sum, the National Energy Plan would aggravate the effects of the energy crisis rather than relieve them: inflation, unemployment, lagging investment, and the threat of economic depression.

It might be argued that all these economic difficulties are the unavoidable cost of solving the energy crisis. This would be true if, as the administration has held, the answer to the crisis is conservation, and the price of energy must be increased in order to encourage conservation. However, this misrepresents the fundamental cause of the energy crisis. The crisis results from our reliance on fuels that are nonrenewable and are therefore certain to increase in price exponentially as long as we continue to produce them. To solve the energy crisis, the cost of producing energy must be stabilized, and the only way to do that is to switch from nonrenewable energy sources to renewable ones. This would eliminate the interactive link that drives the cost of a nonrenewable source exponentially upward, for if an energy source is renewable, producing it has no effect on the accessibility of further supplies.

No matter how much solar energy is used on the earth, there is no effect on the amount that emanates from the sun. When solar energy is used to grow a corn crop this year, it has no influence on the amount of sunlight available for future crops. Thus the difficulty of acquiring a renewable source such as solar energy, and therefore its cost, does not change as it is used (except, perhaps, to decline as devices are improved). Unlike the graph relating the cost of producing a unit of nonrenewable energy to the cumulative amount produced, which curves upward at an ever steeper angle, the graph for a renewable source is a horizontal or gradually falling line. If the energy crisis is to be solved, we must shift from the rising curve to the flat line; we must undertake the transition from nonrenewable energy sources to renewable ones. This is what the National Energy Act failed to do, and in failing it threatens to aggravate the energy crisis rather than resolve it.

5

SOLAR VERSUS NUCLEAR ENERGY:
The Politics of Choice

The political sleight of hand that replaced the National Energy Plan's "cornerstone" (conservation) with a "centerpiece" (natural gas deregulation) is a particularly dramatic example of the confusion that has been the most consistent feature of the energy debate. The fault is pervasive and has affected not only the administration's arguments but in some degree its opponents' as well. The battle over deregulating the price of natural gas, which determined the legislative fate of the Plan, is a good example. Senators Abourezk and Metzenbaum's opposition to deregulation was based on the view that it would accelerate the rising price of energy and add to the economic burden on consumers, especially the poor. Although this view is well justified by the facts, it does not tell us how to meet the need for natural gas, which is just as important to the nation—including consumers and the poor—as a stable price. Because natural gas is nonrenewable, production and price are firmly linked; the cost of producing it, and therefore its price, rise exponentially with continued production. Although profiteering makes matters worse, inevitably, as long as consumers must rely on nonrenewable fuels such as natural gas, they face endless, escalating increases in the cost of energy. Simply opposing deregulation offers no means of breaking this link between price and production. The same is true of energy conservation, which can reduce demand and thus delay the price rise; but again, the link remains and the exponential rise in the price of energy continues.

The only way to solve the problem is to shift to renewable sources of energy that we can keep on producing without forcing the cost of production upward. This is the issue that lies at the heart of the energy crisis. But none of the antagonists in the debate on the National Energy Plan seemed

willing to face it. The debate fumbled about the peripheral issues (price regulation, conservation) as though there was no way to deal with the central one. Yet quite apart from the debate on the Plan, Congress was in fact considering the two existing sources of energy that *are* renewable and could, at least in principle, solve rather than delay the energy crisis—solar energy and breeder-supported nuclear power. But curiously, these discussions avoided the crucial role that these energy sources might play in resolving the crisis. In the topsy-turvy energy debate the peripheral issues were propounded as though they were the heart of the matter, while the truly central issue—the shift to renewable energy sources—remained separate, largely unconnected with the debate on the Plan.

Discussion of the relative merits of solar and nuclear energy was also inverted. Solar energy, the oldest energy source exploited by human society (in the form of windmills, wood, sailing vessels, and agriculture), was usually regarded as an impractical, exotic product of advanced science. Nuclear power—which is, indeed, the product of advanced modern science, and certainly an exotic way to boil water (the basic function of a nuclear reactor is to make steam to drive an electric generator)—was regarded as an unchallengeable, practical reality. This conventional view is reflected in the relative roles of nuclear power and solar energy in the National Energy Plan; nuclear power is supposed to meet 23 percent of the new demand for energy between 1976 and 1985, and solar energy less than 2 percent. But events have stubbornly contradicted this approach, and despite the Plan, the immediate, practical prospects for using solar energy have brightened considerably, while those of nuclear power have dimmed—and, in the aftermath of the accident at Harrisburg, may be extinguished completely. Solar energy is emerging as a potentially creative force in the economy, while nuclear power has become an economic cripple.

The events that were to establish the eminent practicality of solar energy began, without publicity, in a seemingly insignificant, routine legislative event. The occasion was one of the numerous, little-noticed hearings conducted by legislative committees in pursuit of their special responsibilities, in this case the losing battle to help small businesses hold on to their dwindling share of the U.S. economy. On May 13 and 14, 1975, the Senate Select Committee on Small Business, chaired by Senator Gaylord Nelson of Wisconsin, held hearings on the opportunities for small business in solar energy research and development. In opening the hearing, Senator Nelson remarked that the issue was encompassed in three questions:

Solar energy: How much can be converted to human use?
How much can be provided by small business?
How soon?

to which, according to Senator Nelson, the experts and government officials replied:

Not much.
Not much.
Not soon.

The senators heard testimony from small-businessmen, energy experts, and government officials; numerous letters, publications, and reports were submitted for the record. Anyone with the time and patience to read the nearly six thousand pages of overly detailed and often self-serving testimony would be hard pressed to find any discourse that promised to affect seriously the actual course of solar development in the United States. A seemingly typical routine bureaucratic exercise is recorded on page 413 of the Hearings— several hundred pages of testimony bearing the heading: "Statement of Donald B. Craven, Acting Assistant Administrator, Energy Resource Development, Federal Energy Administration, accompanied by Edwin A. Kuhn, Acting Associate Assistant Administrator for Energy Conversion,

FEA; and Norman Lutkefedder, Chief, Solar Energy Branch, Office of Energy Conversion, FEA."

Mr. Craven's prepared statement began with the customary invocation of the national interest ("the present energy situation requires broad, decisive, and prompt government action to prevent continued erosion of our economic vitality"). He continued with an evaluation of how solar energy might contribute to it ("accelerated use of solar energy could allow a substantial savings in the Nation's demand for fossil fuels by 1985"). He then explained what FEA was doing about solar energy ("we are developing, implementing and coordinating programs and policies to facilitate the accelerated utilization and widespread commercial application of proven solar energy technologies").

Legislators have perfected a technique for penetrating such cloudy generalities in order to learn how much effort an agency is actually making to do what it claims to do. A good example is the following exchange:

Senator Hathaway: Mr. Craven, in your statement you indicated the FEA's involvement in solar activity. Could you give us an idea of the budget activity and the staff commitment for this effort?
Mr. Craven: I think I will have Mr. Kuhn speak to that since he is really the supervisor of that effort.
Mr. Kuhn: Mr. Chairman, we have, in the office under Mr. Craven, two full-time professionals dealing with nothing but solar energy at this point.

In answer to the financial question, FEA reported that in the fiscal year 1975 about $200,000 was earmarked for contracts and interagency agreements for research and development on solar energy. At the time, the federal budget for the development of nuclear power was about five thousand times larger—$1 billion.

A casual reader of this record would conclude that FEA was making only a minuscule effort to develop solar energy. A reader better grounded in bureaucratic lore, and perhaps a bit cynical, might conclude as well that the effort was just large enough to justify the inclusion of "Solar Energy Branch, Office of Energy Conversion" in the FEA table of organization, as proof that FEA was doing something about solar energy. Given the size of the staff and budget, not much action to develop solar energy would be expected beyond, perhaps, further testimony at some future hearing.

But this time something did happen. Craven's testimony triggered a chain of events which in two years produced persuasive evidence that solar energy could, at once, begin to solve the energy crisis. There are in Congress some representatives and senators who appreciate the virtues of solar energy and are alert to opportunities to develop it. One of them, Representative Richard L. Ottinger of New York, impressed by FEA's claim that they could "facilitate the accelerated utilization and widespread application of proven solar energy technologies," introduced legislation in the House that would require FEA to draw up detailed plans to back up that claim. Ottinger's effort failed because of a jurisdictional dispute between two House committees over supervision of FEA activities. However, Senators Gary Hart and Charles Percy succeeded in attaching a provision similar to Ottinger's to the Energy Conservation and Production Act (ECPA) of August 1976. Section 110 of the act requires that FEA "develop the policies, plans, implementation strategies and program definitions for promoting accelerated utilization and widespread commercialization of solar energy."

Confronted with this legislative mandate, FEA took steps to carry it out. The Solar Energy Branch staff was increased from two to twenty. It now became a division. A Task Force on Solar Energy Commercialization was set up to carry out the new congressional mandate. Within six months it produced several reports that showed how supposedly "impractical" solar technologies could become economically successful enterprises.

The most spectacular achievement was a commercialization plan for what is usually regarded as the most difficult solar application—the direct production of electricity from sunlight. The Task Force's attack on this problem was a sharp departure from the government's usual approach to the development of energy technology. The conventional approach is device-oriented. The basic idea is to start with some relevant physical principle—for example, that certain materials generate an electric current when exposed to sunlight. Then laboratory experiments are done to discover how the process is affected by various factors. (In the case of light-generated electricity, these would include the composition of the material, the effect of the color and intensity of the light, and of temperature, and the efficiency with which light is converted into electricity.) Following this "research" stage, the program would proceed to "development": small-scale devices would be built and tested to see how well their actual performance matched the theoretical expectations. Finally, in the "demonstration" stage, a full-scale device would be installed, say, on a government building, and its practical performance monitored during different seasons and operational conditions.

In this conventional "R, D & D" process, economic questions are largely ignored until the end. The governing strategy is linear: scientific analysis, technological development, and demonstration proceed, in that order, without considering how the final product might find a place in the national economy. This reflects an assumption, now deeply ingrained in government operations, that the economic feasibility of a new device will be determined—after it has been through the R, D & D process—by the mechanics of the "free market." This would mean, for example, that the production and use of a newly developed solar electric device would depend on whether or not some entrepreneur believed that he could profitably invest in it. To yield a profit, such a device needs to be good enough and cheap enough to compete in the existing market for electricity. At the present time virtually all the electricity generated in the U.S. is produced by large, central power stations fueled by coal, oil, natural gas, or uranium, and according to the conventional approach, the commercial success of a new photoelectric device would depend on how well it could replace these fuels in driving such a central power station. It was this sort of analysis of the practicality of solar energy that led the experts to tell Senator Nelson: "Not much. Not soon." What was needed, according to the government's energy experts, was more research in the hope that a "breakthrough" would yield a new device that could compete economically in the customary market for electric power.

The FEA Task Force took a quite different approach. Instead of concentrating on the device, they looked at the *market* for electricity. They knew that a workable device for converting sunlight into electricity was already available—the photovoltaic cell. This consists of a thin, chemically treated slice of a crystal of silicon (which, together with atoms of oxygen, comprises the molecular structure of common sand). The silicon wafer is mounted on a metal base and covered with a grid of fine wire. When light strikes the top surface of the wafer, an electric current flows between the wire grid and the metal base. The device is silent and motionless; properly protected from the weather, it can last for many years.

By the early 1970s photovoltaic cells were already in small-scale commercial production, and used largely for powering space satellites. In 1976 they were available on the open market at a cost of about $15 per "peak" watt of electricity (that is, the capacity of the device to produce electricity when the sun is at its noontime height). Providing a typical home with 15,000 watts of capacity would cost at least $225,000 for photovoltaic cells, plus the cost of storage batteries (so that power would be available at night or on cloudy days). In contrast, the capital investment needed for conventional central power stations is about $500 to $1,000 per 1,000 watts of capacity (or $7,500 to $15,000 per household). As matters stood, the photovoltaic cell was hardly commercial.

The Task Force set out to find a way of bringing photovoltaic cells into the market despite their current high price. They realized that the existing market for electricity is not uniform; for some uses, electricity costs very much more than what a household or industry pays for it. An extreme example is the dry cell used to operate portable radios, flashlights, and toys, which provides power at a cost of about $20 to $100 per kilowatt-hour, as compared with an average residential electricity cost of $0.035/kWh. Even at its current price a photovoltaic cell can compete quite well against high-priced power from dry cells. A digital watch powered by a photovoltaic cell instead of a depletable dry cell battery is already on the market at a price of about thirty dollars.

However, only a minuscule part of the national production of electricity is generated by dry cells. A more significant part of the market is the high-cost electric power provided by electric generators driven by gasoline or diesel engines, which are used in areas that are remote from power lines. Such generator sets range in size from 100-watt gasoline-driven devices (sold in department stores for use in summer cottages) to diesel-driven generators with capacities of thousands of watts. They are priced at $.20 to $1.00/watt and produce electricity at costs ranging up to $1.63/kWh. If the cost

of photovoltaic cells could be brought down to about $2.00 to $3.00/watt, they could compete effectively with generator sets, and enter at least this part of the electricity market.

One way to reduce the price of a new product is to expand production enough to warrant the introduction of large-scale, efficient factory methods. However, the present market for photovoltaic cells is so limited (production in 1976 amounted to some 350,000 watts) that production methods are small-scale and relatively inefficient. Getting photovoltaic cells into the market is a "bootstrap problem": Because demand is too low to support an efficient scale of production, the cell's price is too high to be competitive; demand is too low because the price is too high.

The FEA team decided to find out if a well-established administrative ploy could break this vicious cycle: a government purchase large enough to finance enlarged, efficient production facilities, which brings the price down and thus opens up new markets that can absorb an expanded supply. This procedure has often been used to create industrial production needed by the government, especially for military equipment. A recent example is the development of the industry that produces "integrated circuits"—postage-stamp-size chips that contain electric circuits sufficiently elaborate to operate complex computer systems. Industrial production of such units began in 1962, based exclusively on Department of Defense orders for military equipment. In that year, about 160,000 units were produced, to be sold at a price of about $50 each. By 1968 annual production had increased to some 120 million units, each costing about $2.50. At that price integrated circuits became cost-effective in many nonmilitary applications, which then took up more than half of the total production. This was the start of the industry that has now produced millions of low-cost hand calculators and digital watches, and computers that regulate everything from TV electronic games to assembly lines. The timely expenditure of public funds created a lively new sector of the private economy.

Perhaps encouraged by this example, the Task Force realized that one of the largest users of generator sets was the Department of Defense. DOD uses generator sets to power remote installations such as radar stations, field telephones, and weather-sensing devices. It appeared that the DOD demand for photovoltaic replacements for these units might be large enough to trigger a substantial expansion of the industry, thus reducing prices enough to warrant the substitution. The Task Force concluded an interagency agreement with the U.S. Army Mobility Equipment Research and Development Command (initially involving a transfer of some $20,000) to analyze the potential market for photovoltaic systems. The command staff ordered a detailed inventory of the DOD's remote power-requiring installations and worked out schemes for using photovoltaic cells to supply them. A survey showed that initially about one-fifth of the existing gasoline-powered generator sets could be replaced by photovoltaic units with a capacity of 152 million watts.

The study then compared the relative cost of existing generator sets and potential photovoltaic replacements. The cost of operating a generator set was computed from the cost of fuel and equipment repairs. The operating cost of a photovoltaic unit was computed from its initial cost and expected longevity, the fuel—sunlight—being free. From such comparisons it was possible to determine the "break-even cost" of photovoltaic cells—that is, the price at which a unit using such cells (and counting the cost of storage batteries and accessory hardware) would be as economical as a conventional generator set of the same capacity. Such calculations showed, for example, that when the price of photovoltaic cells fell below $10/watt, they could be incorporated into replacement units that would be more economical than a conventional 1,500-watt gasoline-driven generator set. In order to substitute economically for a 5,000-watt generator set, the cost of photovoltaic cells would need to be less than $3.70/watt.

With this information in hand, the Task Force estimated the impact of a government order for 152 million watts of photovoltaic cells, to be delivered over a five-year period. One year after the 152-million-watt order was placed, photovoltaic cells would be available at a price of about $2 to $3/watt; after the third year, at about $1/watt; and after the fifth year, at about $.50/watt. This projected twenty-fold price reduction, from $10 to $.50 per watt, is not particularly remarkable. It follows the "learning curve" already experienced by the closely related industry that produces transistors and integrated circuits and is confirmed by commercial estimates of future photovoltaic costs.

Based on this information, the Task Force prepared a "Federal Photovoltaic Utilization Program" for the purchase of 152 million watts of photovoltaic cells, over a five-year period, at a total cost of about $440 million (in 1975 dollars). The cells were to be used to provide solar replacements for about one-fifth of the DOD's gasoline-powered generator sets. The Task Force estimated that this investment would result in net savings of up to $500 million to the federal government over the expected twenty-year life of the cells.

This plan promised to do much more than save the government money. It would also trigger the creation of a new industry capable of producing photovoltaic cells at a cost that would, within a relatively short time, enable these devices to invade a large part of the present market for electricity. Within a year after the start of the program, with the price of photovoltaic cells down to $2 to $3/watt, according to the Task Force report, they would become economical substitutes not only for DOD generator sets, but also for a number of remote power installations used outside the government, such as irrigation pumps and microwave communication repeater stations. This market was estimated at 80 million to 200 million watts. This demand, added to the government's 152-million-watt purchase, would further expand the industry, improve production efficiency, and help to reduce the price even more.

After the third year of the federal purchase plan, when the price of photovoltaic cells reached about $1/watt, they would become economical as replacements for conventional street, highway, and parking lot lighting. (A good deal of the present cost of such lighting is represented by the cables that link the lights to power lines and, of course, by the power itself. Photovoltaic units would eliminate these costs.) Such a unit, mounting a 1,000-watt lamp, might include a vertical panel of photovoltaic cells, about 3 feet by 30 feet, facing south. During the day the electricity generated by the cells would charge a storage battery housed in the base of the unit; at night the stored power would be fed into the lamp. There is a potential market for about 60 million to 90 million of such lighting units, requiring a total of nearly 100,000 million watts of photovoltaic cells. (For comparison, a typical nuclear power plant has a capacity of 1,000 million watts.) When photovoltaic cells are priced at $1/watt, solar units would also become competitive with conventional units for emergency and warning lights for airports and marine installations; power units used to protect pipelines and well casings from corrosion; pumps used for irrigation and similar purposes in developing countries, where power grids are lacking; diesel-driven power generators, ranging from 15 kilowatts to 500 kilowatts in capacity. These applications represent a total market for nearly 150,000 million watts of photovoltaic cells per year. Even a small part of these markets would sustain a considerable further expansion of the industry, and greater reductions in price.

Finally, after the fifth year of the proposed plan, with the price down to $.50/watt, photovoltaic units would begin to compete with conventional systems for residential power, first in the sunny Southwest, but gradually—as the price of conventional electricity continued to rise with the cost of nonrenewable fuels—everywhere in the country. This would open up a market estimated at about 500,000 million watts and would thereby establish photovoltaic cells as a major source of the nation's electric power.

One of the most promising applications of photovoltaic cells would be in developing countries. Most of these countries lack the national electric network, powered by large centralized plants, that is universal in industrialized countries. To build such a system means a massive commitment of capital, which is in short supply in developing countries. If photovoltaic cells were available at a competitive cost, they could be used to supply power to scattered settlements without incurring the huge cost of installing power lines in sparsely settled, remote areas. According to a recent study it would be cheaper, in developing countries, to base an electric supply system on photovoltaic cells rather than on a conventional central station system as soon as the cell cost falls to between $2 to $3 per watt. Recognizing the importance of this option for developing countries, in November 1978 the United Nations offered to purchase 15 million watts of photovoltaic cells from any supplier willing to sell them at $3 per peak watt.

One of the astonishing features of the FEA plan is that the technological improvements in the production of photovoltaic cells that are required to achieve these sharp reductions in cost are almost ludicrously simple. In manufacturing photovoltaic cells, silicon is extensively purified and formed into a cylindrical crystal about two inches in diameter and perhaps a foot long. These ingots are then sawed into wafers about half a millimeter thick. The silicon crystal is extremely hard, so that the saw blade must be very strong, and therefore rather thick. As a result, about half of the silicon ingot is lost as sawdust, and the wafers are thicker than they have to be. One of the big advances proposed by the manufacturers in order to bring down the price of photovoltaic cells is to replace the single thick-bladed saw with one made up of five thin blades (which, together, are as strong as a single thick-bladed saw). With this modification, instead of producing one wafer out of each millimeter of ingot, it will be possible to produce four thinner ones—a considerable saving of very expensive silicon. Some measure of the novelty of this "breakthrough" can be gauged from the fact that a similar technique has been used in the Italian marble industry for many years.

The FEA photovoltaic program is a powerful answer to the common complaint that solar technologies are not now economically competitive in the conventional market for energy, and that only new research "breakthroughs" can make them competitive. The answer is found by turning the problem around: what is improved is not the device, but the market. By finding a segment of the overall market in which photovoltaic cells can already compete, that minimal entry becomes an economic lever to reduce the price of the cells and thus open up new parts of the market—and so on. The process is self-propagating; once it begins, the industry expands, prices fall, and the market for conventional electricity is further invaded. The process is automatic—once it is started by a government purchase.

It is not surprising that such outside intervention should be necessary. Private entrepreneurs are usually unwilling to risk an investment before they are reasonably certain that there is a market for the product. If the market is only a hope, which depends on the successful development of new, expanded production techniques, the enterprise is too risky to compete with more conventional investments and is not likely to be undertaken. As in the case of the integrated-circuit industry, the private economy can benefit considerably, but only after the government—using public funds—makes the initial investment.

Despite its promise, the FEA/DOD study and

the proposal for a federal photovoltaic purchase plan suffered a strange fate. At first glance it would seem to be an idea whose time had come, fortuitously coinciding with the start of a new administration which had pledged, as its first major effort, to create a national program that could solve the energy crisis. But the only reference to this opportunity in the National Energy Plan is rather limited:

> Photovoltaic systems, using cells developed in the space program, are economic today for certain small, decentralized applications. These systems have a potential for dramatic price reductions that would make them economical for a broader range of applications. Increased funding is proposed to accelerate the development of economic photovoltaic systems.

The extent of the administration's commitment to "accelerate the development of economic photovoltaic systems" became clear when the White House opposed legislation for a federal photovoltaic purchase plan. Nevertheless, the purchase plan legislation has been passed as part of the National Energy Act. It involves $98 million rather than the $400 million proposed by the FEA study. The smaller purchase would not do as well as the larger one in reducing the price of photovoltaic cells; it would probably bring the price of photovoltaic cells to $1/watt after five years instead of in three. But it would enable photovoltaic cells to break into the market for electric power, now the exclusive domain of conventional power plants, and to begin the transition to renewable, solar energy.

Wind is another form of solar energy that is ready for commercialization. (Wind is the flow of air displaced by upward movement of air masses which have been heated by the sun, and is therefore a form of solar energy.) Once a familiar part of the rural landscape, windmills were largely abandoned as power from rural electric cooperatives became available, and until recently there has been little interest in improving or building them. However, in the last few years windmill design has been considerably advanced and an infant industry to produce wind-driven electric generators has been started. Modern windmills range in blade size from 15 feet to 150 feet, and in output from 10,000 watts (sufficient for a medium-size household) to 2,500,000 watts (sufficient to

heat and cool a large building or to power a factory).

In response to its congressional mandate, FEA commissioned a study on the commercialization of wind generators by the Mitre Corporation. Although much less detailed than the photovoltaic study, it does show how wind energy can be used, at economically competitive costs, beginning almost at once. Federal expenditures of about $2 billion to $3 billion per year could fund a wind energy program with a capacity of about 20,000 million watts by the mid-1980s and about 100,000 million watts in 2000. The average cost would be about $520/kilowatt, well below even the present costs of nuclear and coal-fired power plants. The program could save as much as 300,000 barrels of oil per day in 1985 and more than 2 million barrels in 2000.

As in the case of photovoltaic cells, the successful commercialization of wind generators depends on fitting them into an economically competitive niche in the present market for electricity. Although wind power does avoid the familiar objection that solar energy is not available at night or in cloudy weather, like sunlight it is intermittent. Therefore, as are all other solar devices, a wind generator is most useful when it is linked to a storage system. Although this adds to the cost and reduces its competitive position, there are ways around the difficulty.

One way to store energy is to use the original source to pump water uphill; when energy is needed, the stored water is allowed to run down through a hydroelectric generator, producing electricity. This technique—pumped storage—is increasingly used by electric utilities to store excess electric power that is generated during periods when demand is low. A good way to minimize the cost of wind-generated electricity is to connect a windmill to the transmission network of a ready-made pumped storage system—a hydroelectric plant. Then, with little added expense, during windy periods power can be used to pump water up into the reservoir, adding to the conventional hydroelectric plant's reserve of power. Such installations, built right now, for example, at the Bonneville Dam, would be cost-effective ways to produce electric power from the sun.

Certain parts of the U.S., such as the Pacific Northwest, where there are many hydroelectric installations, are also rather windy. A study carried out by specialists with the Department of the

Interior has determined that the integration of wind/electric generators and pumped storage sites in seventeen western systems could produce well over 100,000 million watts of electric power, which could be delivered at a cost competitive with the expected cost of power from new nuclear or coal-fired power plants. The cost of such wind-generated power will remain about the same over time, while the cost of conventional power continues to rise exponentially, so that the economic advantage of the solar source is bound to increase.

But again, government intervention is needed. As the study points out: "Bringing wind power to economic maturity will require commitment of major quantities of capital in advance of expected earnings. . . . The past history of innovation suggests that the height of this capital barrier delays commercialization long past the time when it is technically competitive." Experience shows that "commitment of major quantities of capital in advance of expected earnings" can be made only with public funds. Thus, as in the case of photovoltaic cells, the generation of electricity from wind is both technically feasible and economically competitive. It awaits only the investment of funds that are committed to a long-term social return, rather than to short-term private gain.

One form of solar energy—direct heating of water and buildings—needed no further work on the part of the FEA to establish its commercial readiness. This had already been worked out by an early study at the Center for the Biology of Natural Systems (CBNS) and by more elaborate studies commissioned by the National Science Foundation, the Joint Economic Committee of the U.S. Congress, and the Energy Research and Development Administration. Here, too, the solar technology becomes economically competitive only if it is properly integrated into the market—specifically, the present system of water and space heating and the present pattern of financing buildings.

Heating systems that depend *wholly* on solar energy are now economic only in special situations, in which the building is designed with that purpose in mind. In existing buildings of conventional design, the solar source must be combined with the conventional one in a single system. The combined system is more flexible than either one alone. When sufficient sunlight is available to balance the outside temperature, all the needed en-

ergy can be supplied by the sun. On the other hand, on very cold or cloudy days, when sunlight is too weak to match the outside temperature, the system can operate partly or entirely on conventional fuel. In the first case the combined system substitutes free sunlight for expensive fuel or electricity, and in the second it substitutes conventional energy for a costly expansion of the solar system. Because of this flexibility, in most parts of the country a combined system which is about 60 percent solar and 40 percent conventional would provide heat at a minimum cost. Such a system is already competitive with conventional electric heat, and as prices continue to rise it will soon be competitive with natural gas and fuel oil heat.

This emerges from a financial comparison of the two kinds of heating systems. In a conventional system the initial cost of the equipment is relatively small (in a typical one-family home, for a furnace about $2,000 to $4,000, and somewhat less for electric resistance heating), but the householder then faces the relentless escalation of fuel costs into the future. In a solar system the initial cost is high—about $15,000 to $20,000 for a home in the central part of the United States—but the fuel is free and, apart from maintenance, there is no cost for the heat. However, the fixed capital cost of the solar system is usually converted into an annual cost by means of a mortgage, so that it is then represented by the periodic payment on the principal and interest.

A typical example of how these relationships work out in comparison with a home supplied only with electric resistance heat (the most expensive but nevertheless very common residential heat source) is reported in a recent Department of Energy study. The solar part of the system was designed to provide a well-insulated one-family home in Boston with 70 percent of the needed hot water and 50 percent of the space heat (the rest to be provided by conventional electric heat). The solar equipment was financed by a 20 percent down payment and a twenty-year mortgage at 8.5 percent interest. The system would begin to save on heating costs three years after installation and the total savings would equal the down payment in eleven years. With the tax credit provided in the new National Energy Act, the down payment would be recovered in one year if the household is in the 30 percent income bracket. Over the lifetime of the system there would be a net saving of about 20 percent in heating costs.

According to a study by the Mitre Corporation on the economics of such combined solar/electric water and space heating systems, they would today be economical (in comparison with wholly electric resistance systems) in twelve of thirteen representative U.S. cities. The exception is Seattle, where solar collectors cannot compete with the low cost of hydroelectric power—which is itself a renewable solar source. A similar study by the congressional Joint Economic Committee analyzes the feasibility of introducing solar/conventional systems between 1976 and 1990 on a state-by-state basis. Economic feasibility for residential heating begins in the northern states (where conventional fuel costs and yearly heat requirements are high) and moves southward with time. In 1976 it was already economically advantageous to add solar heating to an existing electric (resistance) residential heat system in twenty-six northern and central states. As the price of conventional fuel rises, in 1985 the area of feasibility would extend to Idaho, California, Kansas, Indiana, and West Virginia, and in 1990 to Nevada, Oklahoma, Arkansas, Alabama, Kentucky, and North Carolina. It is out of the running in states such as Washington (which is poor in sunshine and rich in cheap hydroelectric power) and Louisiana, Mississippi, and Florida (which needs too little heat to justify the added investment).

All this is only a sampling of the possible ways of commercializing solar energy. Nevertheless, it shows that for certain uses, such as space heat and hot water, solar energy is already competitive with conventional systems. Recently the Office of Technology Assessment of the U.S. Congress did a systematic study that compared the monthly costs of conventional heat and electricity with those of a wide variety of solar systems. Some five hundred different solar and solar/conventional systems designed for residences and industrial establishments in Albuquerque, New Mexico; Omaha, Nebraska; and Fort Worth, Texas, were evaluated. The results confirm the conclusions from the foregoing sampling, and add the following further information:

Although only mixed solar/conventional systems are now economical for heating a typical residence, in large buildings or groups of houses 100 percent solar systems may now be economical.

By the mid 1980s cost reductions and improvements in photovoltaic cells, in small engines powered from solar sources, and in solar collectors may bring the cost of electricity for residences and commercial buildings to the range of $.04 to $.10/kWh, "a price which would probably be competitive with electricity delivered to these customers from conventional utilities."

In response to the criticism that it is uneconomic for utilities to serve as a backup for solar systems (or to buy the excess power they may produce), the report points out that "Most solar heating systems are equipped with energy storage devices which, at modest additional expense, can be used to reduce or possibly eliminate most adverse effects on electric utilities attributable to solar demand patterns."

Thus there is substantial evidence that certain sources of solar energy—heat from solar collectors and electricity from photovoltaic cells or windmills—either now are or within a few years will be economically competitive with conventional sources of heat and power. However, even the most ardent supporters of solar energy have doubted that it could soon be available, economically, in the other important forms—gaseous and liquid fuel. Such fuels are crucial to the effective operation of a national energy system: liquid fuels are essential for airplanes and for heavy land-based vehicles (such as tractors and construction equipment) that are not readily electrified; gaseous fuel is an important means of transporting energy and, serving as fuel for cogenerators (which produce both heat and electricity), is a major way to save energy. Liquid and gaseous fuels are most readily obtained from the oldest form of solar energy—the organic matter produced, photosynthetically, by green plants—and paradoxically, this is probably the least developed aspect of solar energy at present.

The biological basis for this form of solar energy is, of course, very well known: When plants absorb sunlight, the light-driven photosynthetic system uses part of the absorbed energy to convert carbon dioxide, water, and other inorganic constituents into organic compounds. This is the origin of all natural organic matter—in the tissues of plants and animals; in their organic constituents such as protein, fat, starch, or cellulose; in animal manure and urine. All these materials represent trapped solar energy, which can be released and used—for example, by burning them. They can also be converted into more versatile fuels: for example, by distilling alcohol from grain or fruit that has been fermented by yeast, or capturing the methane (the fuel of natural gas) that bacteria generate from manure, sewage, or garbage. When properly burned, alcohol and methane produce no pollutants; both can be used to run internal combustion engines. They can be produced by old and relatively simple methods. Alcohol can be produced fairly efficiently in either the customary moonshiner's still or the whiskey-maker's factory. Several million simple methane generators have been built in villages in India and China to produce the fuel from animal manure and human sewage. (Such simple sources of solar energy are not always appreciated by some energy experts. For example, during a recent visit to China, Energy Secretary Schlesinger is reported to have remarked, regarding wooden "honey buckets," which are used to save human excrement for methane generation: "The only way to get energy out of those things is to burn them.")

American interest in these sources is recent, but is developing very fast. Farmers are, after all, the last of our true entrepreneurs, alert to new developments and often eager to take advantage of them. They have been painfully aware of the escalating price of the fuel and electricity that they buy, and have begun to generate these energy sources on their own farms, from their own products. A good example is what Archie Zeithamer has recently done. During the summer of 1978, Mr. Zeithamer began to build an alcohol plant on his 500-acre dairy farm near Alexandria, Minnesota. With the help of his family and several neighbors, he assembled the plant from two 4,000-gallon steel tanks (purchased secondhand from a departing gasoline dealer), concrete block, and sundry pipes, pumps, and motors. In October the first batch was started. Ground corn, grown on the farm, was mixed with water, then warmed to break up the grains (using solar energy: a wood fire); an enzyme was added to convert starch to sugar; and then the mixture was fermented by yeast, which yields mash, from which the liquid is separated. After distilling the fermented liquid (again using a wood fire), Zeithamer had produced about 300 gallons of 160 proof (80 percent) ethyl alcohol. The residue from the grain fermen-

tation was fed to the dairy cows and chickens. The entire project cost $16,000, of which $8,000 was for the building to house the equipment. Zeithamer expects to produce 17,000 gallons of 80 percent alcohol per year, which, at current prices, would sell for about $12,000—a remarkably good return on his $16,000 investment. About half of the plant's output will be used on the farm to operate tractors and other farm vehicles. Zeithamer has also used alcohol to operate a cogenerator, thereby converting his own corn to heat and electricity. When Mr. Zeithamer held an open house in October, about 1,500 people toured the plant. Since then 2,500 more people have done so, and he is now helping some of them develop their own alcohol operations.

Near Rice Lake, Wisconsin, another dairy farmer, Len Schieffer, is producing methane from manure. Manure from the dairy barn is transferred to a culvert pipe (of the sort ordinarily used to carry a small stream under a road) 48 feet long and 12 feet in diameter, sealed at both ends. As bacterial action generates methane, the gas is conducted from the top of the culvert pipe into a storage chamber made by placing a large sheet of plastic over a pond. Later the gas is purified by passing it through chemical canisters and stored in a pressurized tank for use. Schieffer uses the methane to drive a cogenerator, which supplies both the farmhouse and the dairy barn with part of their electricity and also supplies heat to the barn.

In Drury, Missouri, Ted Landers is producing methane from spoiled hay and other agricultural waste products and is negotiating with the rural electric cooperative to use it to drive a power generator which will help meet the peak demand for electricity. Throughout the Midwest, farmers are planning large-scale production of alcohol, usually from grain, to be marketed as the gasoline/alcohol mixture (usually 10 percent alcohol) known as "gasohol." In Missouri, a group of farmers has contracted for a $28 million alcohol plant, scheduled to produce 20 million gallons annually; the fermentation residue will be fed to cattle in nearby feed lots. In Colorado, alcohol plants with a total output of nearly 100 million gallons per year are being planned. In Illinois, seventy outlets are already selling gasohol. In Nebraska, a test with state-owned vehicles has shown that gasohol yields about 5 percent better mileage than pure gasoline. (Users also report that gasohol relieves some of the engine performance problems encountered with the new unleaded gasolines.) In some states, recently enacted laws exempt gasohol from fuel excise taxes.

These activities have been encouraged by reports from Brazil, where alcohol production from agricultural products (chiefly derived from sugar cane) is most advanced. The average alcohol content of the total national gasoline supply is already 8 percent. It is expected to rise to 20 percent by 1980 and eventually Brazil intends to use only alcohol to operate automotive vehicles. Tests are under way for using alcohol in turbines to produce electricity in rural areas. Nearly one hundred alcohol plants are now under construction in Brazil.

Activities such as these are usually regarded as of more interest to farmers than to the nation as a whole, on the grounds that they are not likely to add significantly to the huge amount of gasoline, diesel fuel, and jet fuel needed to run the U.S. transportation system. There is some justification for this pessimism about the amount of solar fuels that could be produced from the vegetable matter (usually referred to as biomass) produced in the U.S. Most of the land capable of supporting plants is already used for agriculture and forestry, and at first glance it would appear that any appreciable production of energy from these sources would interfere with the essential production of food, fiber, and lumber. As a result, most estimates of the availability of solar energy from biomass have assumed that only *waste* materials—manure, sewage, and garbage, agricultural, forestry, and cannery wastes—would be used. Relatively small amounts of alcohol and methane could be produced from these sources of biomass. Thus one of the more optimistic assessments of the solar future, the recent report by the Council on Environmental Quality, estimates that biomass sources might yield 3 to 5 quads of energy in the year 2000 and 5 to 10 quads in 2020. These figures do not compare very well with the present (1977) U.S. consumption of natural gas (20 quads) and of liquid fuels for transportation (16 quads). Although conservation measures might cut these requirements in half, a 3 to 5 quad output of fuels from biomass would still fall well short of the need.

If waste biomass is insufficient to produce enough solar fuel, we would need to turn to agricultural crops and timber. But then, it is argued, energy production would reduce food and lumber production. Thus the total energy content of grain, pasture, and hay used to produce livestock in the U.S. (in 1974) is only about 7 quads, which might be expanded to 8 quads if presently idle land was added to the crop acreage. But since all those crops are now used to produce livestock, it is difficult to see how even a few quads of energy could be produced from them without cutting sharply into food production.

However, agriculture is inherently more flexible than one would expect from its present uniformity. In a Corn Belt state such as Illinois, nearly all the farm acreage grows only corn and soybeans, which are in turn used nearly exclusively to raise livestock. However, in the eighteenth century, in areas such as western Pennsylvania, where poor roads made it difficult for farmers to bring crops and livestock to eastern markets, they turned to an equally marketable, but more easily transported, product—whiskey. (It was the effort of the federal government to tax the whiskey, which the farmers regarded as the rightful product of the form of agricultural husbandry mandated by their location, that led to the Whiskey Rebellion in 1794 and later to moonshining.) In those days, the whiskey-makers' "slop"—the wet residue of grain that remained after fermentation—was customarily fed to hogs for local consumption. In modern whiskey-making the grain residue is dried and sold as a livestock feed, "distillers' dried grain." This is a particularly valuable feed because it is richer in protein than the original grain, partly due to the yeast which grows in the mash as it produces alcohol. Thus, quite apart from the value of its obvious product, alcohol fermentation is a very useful way of improving the nutritional value of grain. Sugar beets can also be used; they produce even more alcohol than the same weight of corn, and the residue is a good protein-rich livestock feed.

A recent investigation of these options by a group at CBNS has produced what looks like a conjurer's trick: the same acreage that yields grain and hay with a total energy content of 7 quads per year, which is now totally converted into livestock, can instead be made to produce the same amount of livestock *plus* 8 quads of solar fuel. In this scheme the present acreage in grain/livestock agriculture, expanded by 15 percent to include idle land, would be used to plant a rotation of corn, sugar beets, and hay. Most of the corn and sugar beet crop would be fermented to produce alcohol, and the residue fed to the livestock, together with some hay. This arrangement would provide nourishment for the same amount of livestock that is now produced conventionally, and at the same time yield 5 quads of alcohol—which, in the form of gasohol, will replace about 6 quads of gasoline. The livestock manure and part of the hay crop would be used to produce methane, yielding about 3 quads of that gas. Finally, the residue from methane production would be returned to the land as fertilizer.

This result is not as surprising as it might seem. The present grain/livestock agricultural system was designed for the single purpose of efficiently producing livestock. Now that there is reason to do so, it should be possible to produce *both* food and energy by making full use of the inherent flexibility of agriculture. The task would be far more complex than this brief exercise suggests. Nevertheless, there is reason to believe that eventually agriculture could contribute 8 to 10 quads of alcohol and methane to the national energy budget. About 2 to 3 quads of additional methane probably could be produced from poultry waste, urban garbage, and food-processing wastes. This leaves us with a considerable shortage in methane, which would need to be made up by deliberately producing additional organic matter for that purpose. The most promising source is artificially grown seaweed. According to two recent studies, 10 to 20 quads of methane could be produced from kelp grown on the Pacific coast. Providing that such a new source of methane actually can be realized, it would appear that we need not be too pessimistic about the availability of solar fuels from biomass. If sufficient methane cannot be produced from biomass, then hydrogen (from solar electricity) would need to be added to it.

In a sense, alcohol production has already passed the first test of commercialization: the willingness of entrepreneurs to risk investing in it. It can be argued though that they are likely to lose money, since grain alcohol, which now sells at $1.20 to $1.40 a gallon, is unlikely to replace gasoline that sells at half the price. Most of the present distilleries are old energy-inefficient ones, however. With new energy-efficient distillery designs (some of which use solar fuels to distill the alcohol) and effective marketing of byproduct feeds, the price of biomass alcohol is expected to fall to $1.00 a gallon, or less. If a fuel dealer buys alcohol at $1.00 a gallon, he can produce a gasohol mixture that can be sold in competition with the present cost of regular unleaded or premium unleaded gasoline. Premium unleaded gasoline now costs the dealer about $.53 a gallon. However, he can make a gasohol mixture of equal octane value by mixing nine parts of unleaded regular ($.50 a gallon) with one part of $1.00 alcohol. This brings the dealer's cost to about $.55 per gallon. The recently enacted Federal Energy Act provides for a $.04 per gallon tax credit on each gallon of gasohol. Thus, the dealer's actual cost is $.51 per gallon, making gasohol competitive with premium unleaded gasoline. In those states that have exempted gasohol from the gasoline tax, the dealer's cost is further reduced by $.04 to $.05 per gallon and gasohol becomes competitive with regular unleaded gasoline. Thus, gasohol is already just about competitive with premium unleaded gasoline, and in some states with regular unleaded gasoline. Finally, the OPEC action to raise 1979 oil prices, added to the expected price increases already enacted by the government, will raise gasoline prices by at least $.15 a gallon and bring gasohol well beyond the point of competing successfully with gasoline. And since the price of all nonrenewable fuels will continue to rise, it would appear that the farmers who are investing in alcohol production can expect to turn a profit in 1979, which will increase year by year thereafter.

The key to such a solar success is not some "exotic" new process or device, but simply the judicious integration of long-known agricultural and technological processes: the production of alcohol by fermentation of grains and sugary plant products; livestock feeds derived from fermentation residue; methane production from manure.

But solar energy is not only a technical matter; it has various cultural, ethical, and emotional connotations as well. Some people favor solar energy because, unlike gasoline or nuclear power, it is "natural"; others favor it because solar devices can be small, or even hand built. There has been some tendency, therefore, to regard any way of producing solar energy as inherently good. It turns out, however, that solar energy is not a panacea; it is entirely possible to devise ways of producing and using solar energy that are likely to do more harm than good, at least economically, and in some cases physically.

This brings us to a group of solar technologies that have thus far not figured in this discussion.

These include ocean thermal systems, which use the temperature difference between deep, cold ocean waters and the sun-warmed surface waters to generate electric power; solar power stations, in which a field of mirrors concentrates intense solar radiation on a boiler, producing steam which drives an electric generator; a solar satellite, in which a huge array of photovoltaic cells produces electricity which is beamed (in the form of microwave radiation) to a collecting station on the earth's surface for distribution. These solar technologies are usually also given a prominent place in conventional discussions of solar energy. With a kind of technological democracy, equal consideration is given to modest, long-established technologies—a $500 slow-burning wood stove or a $15,000 grain-alcohol plant—as to an enormously expensive, totally untried device such as a solar satellite, which might cost upward of $100 billion.

Such a seemingly open-minded approach obscures the importance of the most distinctive feature of solar energy—that it is diffusely spread across the entire surface of the planet. Any solar device that is large and centralized—such as a central solar power station or a solar satellite—is *inherently* uneconomic. This emerges from a fundamental difference between solar energy devices and conventional ones. Such forms of conventional equipment as power plants have steadily become larger and more centralized, as have the power grids needed to distribute the electricity they produce. There is a sound economic reason for this trend: the larger the power plant, the less costly the power it produces. This "economy of scale" is so large as to overcome the cost of the added power transmission lines, which must, of course, accompany the increase in plant size (transmission lines now represent more than half the total cost of centralized power systems). Therefore, it is economically sensible to centralize the power source, and to incur the high cost of transmission, *only if* there is a considerable economy of scale in the power plant itself.

However, unlike conventional energy sources, *there is no economy of scale in the acquisition of solar energy.* Since sunlight falls everywhere, an installation is enlarged simply by expanding the area over which the light is received—whether by mirrors for a central power boiler, by collectors for a space heat system, by photovoltaic cells for an electric power system, or by corn plants for producing grain. Each mirror, solar collector, photovoltaic cell, or corn plant is as efficient as the next one. Therefore, a large assemblage of such units is just as efficient as a small one; there is no economy of scale. As a result, a large, centralized solar plant produces energy no more cheaply than a small one (apart from minor savings in maintenance costs). Thus, with transmission costs eliminated or at least greatly reduced, the small plant is by far the more efficient way to deliver the energy. This means that the present pattern of building huge, centralized power stations is *inherently* uneconomical if it is applied to solar energy. No future technical "breakthrough" can overcome this fact.

Unhappily, this fairly simple piece of common sense may elude the most expert of analysts. A case in point is the recent report of the American Physical Society Study Group on Solar Photovoltaic Energy Conversion. The study, which was jointly funded by the Office of Science and Technology Policy of the Executive Office of the President and the Department of Energy, is a very elaborate comparison of the cost of conventional electricity and the cost of electricity produced by *central* photovoltaic installations. In a list of some 175 references, the study fails to include the FEA commercialization study. Indeed, the study makes no comparisons of the conventional electric system with *decentralized* photovoltaic designs. By choosing to saddle the photovoltaic approach with precisely the wrong sort of design, it becomes relatively easy to demonstrate that "It is unlikely that photovoltaics will contribute more than 1% of the U.S. electrical energy produced near the end of the century."

Nevertheless, a very large part of the government's minuscule effort to develop solar energy is devoted to precisely those solar devices that slavishly imitate the design of conventional, centralized power sources. A prominent example is the centralized solar power plant now being built with the joint support of DOE and a local utility at Barstow, California. A benign view of this trend is that it is a modern example of the kind of cultural lag that impelled the first clay potters to imprint the design of the earlier woven vessels on their pots, or the producers of plastic automobile upholstery to ornament it with pseudo stitches. A more cynical view is that such experiments are designed to fail and to demonstrate that solar energy is uneconomical, leaving the way open to the adoption of the alternative route to a system of renewable energy—breeder-based nuclear power.

Perhaps the final irony in the solar energy story is that while it has been treated like a technological orphan by the U.S. government and the major U.S. industries, elsewhere—notably in Italy—solar energy may become a technological Cinderella. Thus, while Mr. Carter, with the help of the American Physical Society Study Group, was throwing cold water on photovoltaic cells, in Italy the huge Montedison industrial complex formed a $10 million joint venture with one of the few U.S. photovoltaic cell manufacturers, Solarex Corporation of Rockville, Maryland, which will manufacture solar panels and photovoltaic devices at a new plant in Florence for Italian and Middle Eastern markets. The factory is expected to produce 3 million watts of photovoltaic cells annually (present U.S. production is considerably less than half a million watts). And while in March 1979 U.S. energy officials anguished over how we would meet an expected oil deficit of 2 to 3 percent due to the cutback in Iranian production, and oil companies were already promising less fuel at higher prices, just one year earlier this item appeared in the trade paper, *Solar Energy Intelligence Report:*

ITALY—Two Italian solar firms have won an International Energy Agency bid for a 500-kilowatt (electric) plant to be constructed in Almeria, Spain. Finmeccanica-Ansaldo and ENI-Snamprogetti groups won the bids over American and European competitors. Ansaldo groups will use its "concetratori distribuiti" system for delivery of heat energy to a ground power generator, and the ENI group will be responsible for testing, quality control, and maintenance. Leader in international solar development, the Ansaldo group sold a mirror-power unit one year ago to the Georgia Institute of Technology, has other American sales in progress and is a major contractor on a European Community solar electric plant in Sicily.

Christian Democrats are backing a Communist party bill which calls for a series of tax and subsidy incentives for home heating and electric power. Italian government research agency recently estimated that a massive program of incentives could give solar plants a major share of energy supply capability in 10 years. Italian Communist Party spokesman Luciano Barca said that conversion on this scale could save 14.6% per year on imports of petroleum, gas, coal and other energy. "We are not an all nuclear party," said Barca in supporting the plan for decentralized home solar heating and electrical units.

In the last few years, the commercial prospects of the two sources that in theory could support the transition to renewable energy—solar energy and breeder-based nuclear power—have moved in opposite directions. It has become clear that, while solar energy could now rapidly invade the energy market, nuclear power is losing ground. Even its supporters despair for its future. In November 1977, John O'Leary, Deputy Secretary of Energy, said that if we continue with the *status quo,* "the nuclear option is dead." And, in fact, since then it may have died at Harrisburg.

A chief reason for such despair is that the economic performance of the nuclear power industry has been very disappointing. The industry has failed to achieve the economic goal that has been its main justification—the production of cheap electric power. Data reported by the industry's chief proponent, the Atomic Industrial Forum, show that on the average the marginal cost of electricity produced by new nuclear power plants in 1976 was about 20 percent higher than the cost of power from new coal-fired plants. Public utilities have been sharply cutting back new orders for nuclear power plants, which fell from thirty-four in 1973 to an annual average of four in 1975–77. In 1978 only two new plants were ordered and a number were canceled. And the plants that have been constructed have performed poorly, costing more to build and operating less reliably than expected. As a result, although the Atomic Energy Commission had predicted that nuclear power would produce 12 percent of the nation's electricity by 1975, the actual figure was only 9 percent. And with the rapid decline in new orders since 1973, the predicted figure of 33 percent for 1985 is clearly already out of reach. In addition, presently operating reactors continue to suffer from safety defects, which, for example, caused the NRC to shut down five reactors in the beginning of 1979.

Perhaps the most persuasive evidence of the failure of the nuclear power industry comes from the business community. Saunders Miller, a prominent utilities investment adviser who has thoroughly examined the business potential of the industry, analyzed the economic impact of the numerous risks that affect an investment in a nuclear power plant. These include their high capital costs, which always greatly exceed the initial estimates; their unreliability; the growing scarcity and rising price of uranium fuel; economic and operational risks in fuel reprocessing; security problems. Miller's final evaluation of the wisdom of investing in nuclear power plants is devastating:

> ... the conclusion that must be reached is that, from an economic standpoint alone, to rely upon nuclear fission as the primary source of our stationary energy supplies will constitute economic lunacy on a scale unparalleled in recorded history, and may lead to the economic Waterloo of the United States.

One of the chief manufacturers of nuclear power plants, General Electric, has announced a reorganization of its nuclear division, which the *Wall Street Journal* interpreted as a preparatory step toward closing down its nuclear power plant section if profits failed to materialize.

Nevertheless, the Carter administration has made a strong effort to revive the dying industry by proposing legislation that would limit environmental challenges to new plants. The administration's intense interest in expanding the role of nuclear power comes as a surprise to those citizens who remember Mr. Carter's declaration, during the election campaign, that nuclear power is a "last resort," a position he has reiterated in subsequent public statements. However, his more private statements have been different. In a meeting in April 1978 with executives of the nuclear industry and the building trade unions (to endorse a no-strike pledge in the construction of nuclear power plants), Mr. Carter announced his strong support for rapid construction of nuclear power plants—but only after he had asked reporters to leave the room. Dr. Schlesinger has been more forthright and has proclaimed that nuclear power "is enshrined in the President's program." It is. If the Plan is carried out, nuclear power would account for nearly one-fourth of the new energy produced between 1976 and 1985.

For many Americans the Plan's emphasis on nuclear power elicits the terrifying prospect of a nuclear catastrophe. The argument over the safety of nuclear power plants is not new, but in 1977 it broke out of the narrow precincts of environmentalism into the broad arena of public affairs. At Seabrook, New Hampshire, nearly two thousand people from all over New England, with the support of townspeople, occupied the site of a new nuclear power plant. Most of them were arrested. Nevertheless, the idea spread from the New England Clamshell Alliance in the East to the Great Plains Alliance in the Midwest and the Abalone Alliance in California. In August 1977 there were more than one hundred anti-nuclear demonstrations all across the country. In June 1978 twenty thousand people massed near the Seabrook site to protest its construction. That November, in a surprising political upset, the Governor of New Hampshire, Meldrim Thomson (who had made much over his support for the nuclear plant), was defeated in a bid for reelection.

A good deal of this opposition to nuclear power plants was based on concern over the hazards of their intensely radioactive wastes. In the absence of a "disposal" procedure that can isolate them from people and the environment over the 100,000-to-200,000-year period in which they will remain dangerous, the wastes have been stored in temporary places. The federal government's effort to find long-term storage sites has met considerable resistance from local populations and state governments. Several states, among them California, Iowa, Maine, Wisconsin, and Montana, have banned the construction of new nuclear power plants until this issue is resolved. Opposition to nuclear power has become a fact of political life in the United States, as it has in Sweden (where the Social Democrats lost power for the first time in forty-four years and the succeeding coalition broke up over the issue); in France (where an anti-nuclear "ecology party" got nearly 10 percent of the votes in the last election); in West Germany (where occupation of reactor sites literally brought the country's nuclear program to a standstill); in Spain (where 150,000 people came to protest the construction of a nuclear power plant near Bilbao); in Italy (where an intense political debate has forced a sharp reduction in the government's nuclear plans); in Austria (where despite the prime minister's opposition, a recent referendum forbade the operation of that country's first completed nuclear power plant, constructed at a cost of some $650 million); in Iran (where the Shah was forced, by his political opponents, to cancel all but two of twenty planned nuclear power plants).

The accident at the Three Mile Island Nuclear Power Plant in March 1979 is certain to intensify this opposition, and not only in the United States. (In direct response to the accident, the government of the city of Montalto di Castro, Italy—a coalition of the Communist, Socialist, and Republican parties—voted to demand that the construction of Italy's largest nuclear power plant, near that city, be stopped, and Sweden is preparing a referendum on the issue.) Even from the sketchy information that was available about the accident shortly after it happened, it was clear that the event confirmed the view that because of its very design nuclear power is an *inherently* dangerous technology. The high and growing cost of nuclear power plants is due not so much to the difficulties associated with the technology that it has in common with non-nuclear plants—that is, the conversion of energy of steam into electricity—but rather to its unique feature, the use of fission to supply the heat needed to produce steam. The accident at Harrisburg showed that a failure in the steam-to-electricity section of the plant that would have caused very little trouble in a conventional power plant came close to producing a catastrophic disaster in the nuclear one and has shut down the plant for a long time, and possibly permanently.

The Three Mile Island Power Plant produced the steam needed to drive its electric turbines in a pressurized-water reactor. In such a reactor, water is circulated through the reactor's fuel core, where—because it is under pressure—it is heated far above its normal boiling point by the heat generated by the fission reaction. The superheated water flows through the reactor's "primary loop" into a heat exchanger where it brings water, which circulates in a "secondary loop," to the boiling point, and the resulting steam flows into the turbine to generate electricity. The spent steam is recondensed and pumped back to the heat exchanger, where it is again converted to steam, and so on. A third loop of cooling water is used to condense the steam, carrying off the excess heat to a cooling tower where it is finally released into the air. This arrangement is much more complex than the design of a conventional power system, where the steam generated in the boiler passes directly into the turbine. In this type of nuclear plant the water that circulates through the reactor (which is equivalent to the boiler in a conventional plant) becomes intensely radioactive, and the complex successive circulation loops are essential to keep that radioactivity from leaving the reactor.

On March 28, 1979, at 3:53 a.m., a pump at the Harrisburg plant failed. Because the pump failed, the reactor's heat was not drawn off in the heat exchanger and the very hot water in the primary loop overheated. The pressure in the loop increased, opening a release valve that was supposed to counteract such an event. But the valve stuck open and the primary loop system lost so much water (which ended up as a highly radioactive pool, six feet deep, on the floor of the reactor building) that it was unable to carry off all the heat generated within the reactor core. Under these circumstances, the intense heat held within the reactor could, in theory, melt its fuel rods, and the resulting "meltdown" could then carry a hugely radioactive mass through the floor of the reactor. The reactor's emergency cooling system, which is designed to prevent this disaster, was then automatically activated; but when it was, apparently, turned off too soon, some of the fuel rods overheated. This produced a bubble of hydrogen gas at the top of the reactor. (The hydrogen is dissolved in the water in order to react with oxygen that is produced when the intense reactor radiation splits water molecules into their atomic constituents. When heated, the dissolved hydrogen bubbles out of the solution.) This bubble blocked the flow of cooling water so that despite the action of the emergency cooling system the reactor core was again in danger of melting down. Another danger was that the gas might contain enough oxygen to cause an explosion that could rupture the huge containers that surround the reactor and release a deadly cloud of radioactive material into the surrounding countryside. Working desperately, technicians were able to gradually reduce the size of the gas bubble using a special apparatus brought in from the atomic laboratory at Oak Ridge, Tennessee, and the danger of a catastrophic release of radioactive materials subsided. But the sealed-off plant was now so radioactive that no one could enter it for many months—or, according to some observers, for years—without being exposed to a lethal dose of radiation.

Some radioactive gases did escape from the plant, prompting the Governor of Pennsylvania, Richard Thornburgh, to ask that pregnant women and children leave the area five miles around the plant. Many other people decided to leave as well, and within a week 60,000 or more residents had left the area, drawing money from their banks and leaving state offices and a local hospital shorthanded.

Like the horseshoe nail that lost a kingdom, the failure of a pump at the Three Mile Island Nuclear Power Plant may have lost the entire industry. It dramatized the vulnerability of the complex system that is embodied in the elaborate technology of nuclear power. In that design, the normally benign and easily controlled process of producing steam to drive an electric generator turned into a trigger for a radioactive catastrophe.

Even if it is ever possible to resolve these troubles, the nuclear power industry, in its present configuration, cannot support the transition to a renewable energy system. Present (light-water) reactors are fueled with natural uranium, and can operate only as long as this fuel is available at some reasonable cost. But natural uranium is a nonrenewable fuel and recent estimates indicate that if present plans for the development of nuclear power were carried out, useful uranium supplies would be exhausted, both in the U.S. and in the world, in about twenty-five to thirty years. Nuclear power can sustain a renewable energy system capable of solving the energy crisis only if it is based on breeder reactors, in which the nuclear reaction is so arranged as to produce new fuel as the reactor generates power. If the planned-for U.S. nuclear power system is based on breeders, the supply of fuel will be enough to support appreciable nuclear power production for perhaps 1,500 to 2,000 years. But before that can happen, nuclear power will need to survive the growing challenge to both its economic and its political viability.

This, then, is the recent history of the two forms of energy on which our hopes for the future now rest. One, solar energy, which has been held back by official neglect, is an old technology ready to cross the threshold of economic viability. The other, nuclear power, which has been heavily supported by public and private funds, is a new technology that—if it survives its troubled infancy—seems already to have lapsed into economic senility. If the present state of the energy problem is intolerable, its future seems uncertain. Yet, somehow, we must negotiate the historic passage between them.

6

THE SOLAR TRANSITION:
The Politics of Transformation

As we have seen, the basic reason for the energy crisis is that nearly all the energy now used in the United States (and in the world) comes from nonrenewable sources. As a nonrenewable energy source is depleted, it becomes progressively more costly to produce, so that continued reliance on it means an unending escalation in price. This process has a powerful inflationary impact: it increases the cost of living, especially of poor people; it aggravates unemployment; it reduces the availability of capital. No economic system can withstand such pressures indefinitely; sooner or later the energy crisis *must* be solved. And this can be done only by replacing the present nonrenewable sources—oil, natural gas, coal, and uranium—with renewable ones, which are stable in cost. That is what a national energy policy must do if it is to solve the energy crisis, rather than delay it or make it worse. But this is a little like saying that all we need to do to cure the ills of earthly life is to enter Paradise. The real problem is whether it is possible to get there from here, and if so, how. The problem is one of transition.

To begin with, it is useful to ask what possible sources of energy might support such a new, renewable system. In theory there are three: solar energy, breeder-based nuclear power, and fusion power. (In a fusion reactor, energy is generated by bringing about the fusion of two atoms of heavy hydrogen, which is available from surface waters in such huge amounts as to be, in effect, inexhaustible over any reasonable span of time.) To be capable of supporting a future, renewable system, an energy source must first meet a rather rudimentary test: it should exist. It is not enough to hope, or even to expect, that a renewable energy source might become available sometime in the future. We must be certain of it, now. This requirement reflects two basic features of the en-

ergy crisis: the crucial, irreplaceable role of energy in production, and the need to begin, at once, to combat the already considerable economic effects of reliance on nonrenewable sources. To embark, today, on a transition to a nonexisting but hoped-for renewable energy source would be like building a bridge across a chasm without first locating the other side. The consequences of failure are simply too devastating to allow for such a risk in a national energy policy.

This requirement eliminates fusion from consideration, for however promising the current research to achieve this source of power may be, it has not yet succeeded. We can neither wait for the experiments to succeed nor take the risk involved in embarking, now, on a transition that depends on their future success. Moreover, although, if it succeeded, fusion power might reduce the massive long-lasting radioactive wastes produced by present nuclear reactors and breeders, it would nevertheless share some of their undesirable features. Some radioactivity would be created, most of it in the especially dangerous form of radioactive hydrogen, tritium; fusion power plants would necessarily be very large and demanding of capital, and therefore economically inefficient.

We are left, then, with the two existing sources of renewable energy that might replace the present nonrenewable ones: breeder-based nuclear power and solar energy. Whichever of these directions the transition to renewable energy takes, it must meet several stringent requirements. Paramount among them is efficiency—with respect to both energy and the considerable amounts of capital involved in producing and using energy. Energy is uniquely capable of yielding work, which is, in turn, essential to the production of all goods and services. Energy is therefore essential to the generation of economic output. But the production and use of energy also withdraw from that output the capital needed to build the machines that produce energy and derive work from it. The economic benefit that can be gained from energy therefore depends on how efficiently both the energy and the capital are applied to the work-requiring tasks of production.

The present system is very inefficient in its use of both energy and capital. No more than about 15 percent of the work that could be gotten out of the energy consumed in the U.S. is actually applied to the work-requiring tasks. And the productivity of capital in energy production—the amount of energy produced per dollar of capital invested—has been declining. Energy production has been taking up an increasing fraction of the capital available for business investment—a figure that is likely to reach about one-third in the next decade. Unless these efficiency figures are improved, the transition, which will be difficult and expensive under the best of circumstances, might become nearly unattainable. The transition to renewable energy is supposed to relieve an intolerable strain on the economic system; but it is unlikely to succeed in that purpose unless the new, renewable energy system, as well as the transitional process that leads to it, is efficient and thrifty.

If an energy system is to be even moderately efficient, energy must be applied to each work-requiring task in a form that is appropriate to that task. The chief work-requiring tasks are: heating and cooling; operating moving but stationary devices, such as home appliances and factory and farm equipment; providing heat for industrial processes; operating land-mobile vehicles, such as cars, trucks, tractors, and trains; operating aircraft; lighting; communication. The efficiency of the match between these tasks and the various forms of energy is governed by some very rudimentary considerations, as well as rather subtle ones. For example, although light can be obtained by burning a liquid or gaseous fuel—or for that matter even wood—electric lamps are so vastly superior that electricity has become the exclusive source of energy for this task. Similarly, for simple, physical reasons airplanes can be driven only by liquid fuels, such as gasoline or kerosene (jet fuel). Solid fuels (such as coal or wood) and the cumbersome machines needed to convert their energy into motion are too heavy. Although a conventional airplane engine could be operated on gaseous fuels (such as natural gas or methane),

they are so light as to require huge storage tanks, far too large to fit in an airplane. Natural gas equivalent in energy content to jet fuel would be nearly one thousand times its volume at sea-level pressure. The gas could be liquefied by cooling, but then it would need to be contained in heavy insulated tanks. If an airplane used electricity, it would need to carry batteries about three hundred times heavier than the equivalent amount of jet fuel, and it would hardly do to tether an airplane to a power plant with a long electric cord. In land-based vehicles such simple, physical problems are less severe. Although liquid fuels offer the best combination of energy content, weight, and bulk, with some inconvenience a car or truck can operate on a solid fuel or a gas. During World War II, in European countries, where conventional fuels were scarce, some truck engines used methane generated in charcoal-burning trailers, and some cars used methane stored in large roof-mounted gas bags. Trains, of course, operated for a long time on coal, or even wood.

However, all these burnable fuels are, in fact, very poorly matched to the task of generating a vehicle's motion, and they are inherently inefficient when used for that purpose. Here the efficiency of the match is governed by the subtleties of the second law of thermodynamics. This law limits the fraction of the fuel's heat that can possibly be converted to motion: about 40 percent in engines such as those that drive vehicles or power plants. Thus a fuel-driven automobile, truck, or train, operating at its highest possible thermodynamic efficiency, could convert considerably less than half of the energy contained in its fuel into motion; the remaining energy would be ejected, as heat, and would merely warm up the surroundings, to no useful purpose. (The efficiency of vehicles is actually much lower; usually only 20 percent of the fuel energy is converted to motion.) The appropriate, most efficient form of energy for driving vehicles is electricity. Electricity is itself a form of motion (moving electrons) and it can be converted into the rotation of a motor and, in turn, into the motion of a vehicle with nearly 100 percent efficiency.

However, if such high levels of efficiency are to be realized in powering not only land-based vehicles but also the numerous moving but stationary devices used in homes, offices, and factories, the production of electricity must itself be maximally efficient. Here the 40 percent limit imposed by the second law again enters the picture: because of it, most of the energy in the fuel used by an electric power plant is not converted to electricity but is ejected into the environment as heat. If that heat is wasted, then despite the nearly perfect efficiency with which electricity is converted to the motion of a kitchen appliance or an electrified train, the *overall* process will waste much more of the fuel's energy than it uses. In the present U.S. energy system, nearly every electric power plant operates in just this way, so that most of the energy available from the fuel that is now used to generate electricity is wasted, as rejected heat.

When there is a mismatch between the form of energy and the task to which it is devoted, capital as well as energy is wasted. With every unnecessary increment in the demand for energy, increasing amounts of capital must be used to produce it, as oil and gas wells go deeper and more expensive recovery methods are used. In electric power production, the efficiency with which capital is used in the production of energy also depends on the plant's size. Apart from a few very large industrial operations (such as aluminum refining and the production of nuclear fuel), most of the demand for electricity is composed of numerous widespread units—homes, stores, office buildings, factories, and farms. If power is generated at a large, centralized plant, the utility must transmit electricity over correspondingly long distances in order to reach its scattered customers. Long power lines demand considerable capital, which in the present U.S. system is even more than the capital invested in power plants. In addition, a good deal of energy is lost, as heat, in electric transmission, amounting to about 10 percent in the present U.S. power network.

In such a highly centralized power system, the economy of scale achieved by the power plant more than compensates for the extra transmission costs. However, when a power plant is very large, the power system as a whole suffers from another type of inefficiency, which cannot be compensated. This problem arises from the difficulty of matching the system's power-producing capacity to the demand for power. Demand for electricity is generated by very large numbers of individual power-driven units (toasters, vacuum cleaners, streetlights, industrial motors, and so forth) and therefore increases only gradually, in many small steps. If the rising demand must be met by building single, large power plants (a typi-

cal power plant has about one million times the capacity needed to operate a toaster), capacity will rise in a series of abrupt, very big steps. For a time after such a large new plant is put into operation, the system will necessarily have a greater capacity than is needed to meet the demand. Eventually, when the gradually rising demand begins to catch up with capacity, another large plant will be built, again producing a sudden excess in capacity over demand, and so on. Inevitably, for a good part of the time the system has more capacity than it needs. Overcapacity means that more capital is invested in the system than is actually needed to meet the demand, a serious source of economic inefficiency. (Difficulty in raising capital is perhaps the utilities' most serious problem at present.) And if an effort is made to cure overcapacity by sending some of the power to another system which is short of capacity, the added transmission is especially costly in both energy and capital.

Finally, the overall efficiency of an energy system depends a great deal on how far the energy is transmitted, and in what form. When energy is moved from the place where it is produced to a place where it is used, some of it is uselessly dissipated as heat. Generally, the energy lost in transmission is related to the resistance in the system which must be overcome to move the energy. In turn, this depends on the form of the energy. Thus it takes more energy to push thick oil than a thin gas through a pipeline. Such differences are reflected in the relative cost of transmitting different forms of energy (which includes both the energy used in transmission and the capital and operating costs of transmitting it). Gas is the most easily delivered fuel; its delivery cost is about $.85 per million BTU, as compared with $4.16 for electricity and $5.27 for hot water. Heat (usually transmitted as steam or hot water) is in a class by itself; so much of it is lost in transmission that only short transmission distances—usually ten miles or less—are practical.

Another requirement that ought to be met by any newly developed energy system is that it should improve the poor quality of the environment. The production and use of energy accounts for a large part of our environmental problems: oil spills; the environmental hazards of coal and uranium mining, for miners as well as the general public; automotive smog; nuclear radiation; unsightly, and possibly harmful, high-tension power lines; the long-term effect of carbon dioxide on the earth's heat balance. In judging the suitability of alternative sources of renewable energy, it is important to compare their relative effects on such environmental problems.

The transition to a renewable energy system must also meet a final requirement: it must be smooth and uninterrupted. What happened in the bitter winter of 1976–77 is a useful cautionary tale. Large areas of the Midwest ran out of natural gas that winter because producers in Texas preferred to make an extra profit by selling gas within the state rather than ship it north through the pipelines at a regulated, lower price. The result was massive economic dislocation. Factories shut down, thousands of people were thrown out of work, schools and government services were disrupted. The resultant economic loss was probably many times larger than the extra profit on the missing fuel. This is a warning that energy is so vital to production that a serious break in its flow could bring the country's economy to a halt.

Thus there is a basic dilemma inherent in the replacement of the present, nonrenewable fuels by renewable ones. Although the continued use of nonrenewable fuels involves very grave threats to the national economy, any interruption in their flow would be even more disastrous. We face a paradox of the sort that Zen masters use to test their pupils: If we cannot very well continue to live with these fuels, and cannot, right now, live without them, what is to be done? The answer is to continue our reliance on the present fuels, but with a new emphasis on those fuels and ways of using them that facilitate their gradual replacement by renewable energy sources. The present, nonrenewable fuels must somehow provide a bridge to the new, renewable ones that must replace them. Thus the transition involves not only the development of sufficient supplies of renewable sources of energy, but also, at an even earlier stage, decisions about how the present, nonrenewable sources are to be produced and used. In particular, one or more of the present energy sources must be used as a "bridging fuel," to facilitate the entry of the new, renewable sources.

At first glance, a transition toward renewable, breeder-based nuclear power seems simple, because these power plants, like ordinary nuclear reactors, produce energy in only a single, particu-larly useful form—electricity. They also produce much larger amounts of heat, but since heat is hard to transport over long distances, and both breeders and conventional nuclear plants are too dangerous for proximity, it is difficult to use. Instead, the heat is ejected into the environment, as a stressful waste. Only those few industrial establishments that might be willing to tolerate a close nuclear neighbor, and need the waste heat, might take advantage of its availability. There have been few takers, and, after the accident at Harrisburg, there are likely to be even fewer. For the reasons already cited (the need to isolate and protect breeders and other nuclear plants, and their considerable economy of scale), the plants would be very large and centralized, and the power distribution network correspondingly large and expensive. A recent proposal for a breeder-based power system in the United States visualizes some 1,000 power plants, each about 1,000 million watts in capacity and costing about $3.4 billion. In comparison, the present U.S. nuclear power system consists of 70 plants, averaging about 730 million watts in capacity and costing about $450 million each. With the introduction of breeders, the present power system would become greatly expanded, more centralized, and considerably more expensive.

Since the useful energy available from a nuclear breeder system would be almost entirely in the form of electricity, all the nation's energy-requiring tasks—in effect, the entire production system—would have to be driven electrically, or by fuels produced from electricity. Most of the energy-requiring tasks now supplied by direct combustion of fuels would have to be redesigned to accommodate electric power. Instead of being heated by oil or natural gas, homes and commercial establishments would have to be equipped with electric heaters or, better, with electric heat pumps, which are more efficient. Gasoline- and diesel-driven cars, trucks, and tractors would have to be replaced by electric vehicles and by electrified railroads. Where a liquid fuel is absolutely essential—for example, in airplanes—it would have to be produced electrically, perhaps by using electricity to generate hydrogen, from which the more conventional hydrocarbon fuels could then be synthesized. Those industries that now burn oil, natural gas, or coal would have to switch to electrical heaters or to liquid fuels produced electrically. In agriculture, similar changes would have to be made to provide heat for drying grain and other crops. Thus, because the single energetic output of a nuclear breeder system—electricity—does not match the varied forms of energy that are used in industrial and agricultural production and in transportation, the introduction of this system would require extensive changes in present energy-using production equipment, at considerable additional cost.

The very large size of the breeder reactors, and the highly centralized design of the power system, would cause serious inefficiencies. Because plants would be distant from consumers, transmission energy losses would be high. Because each power plant would be very large, there would be a great disparity between capacity and demand, so that capital would be wasted. Finally, because breeder reactors are inherently dangerous, and must therefore be isolated, the heat they generate would largely go to waste, and the entire system would be much bigger—and more expensive—than it would have to be if it were sufficiently benign to permit heat-using industries and residences to settle nearby.

In a transition to a breeder-based renewable energy system, two present, nonrenewable sources could serve as bridging fuels: uranium and coal. It would make sense to expand the present system of light-water nuclear reactors, which use uranium, because the spent fuel can be reprocessed to yield plutonium—a breeder fuel. Also, the expanded facilities for reprocessing nuclear fuel and for disposing of radioactive waste would be needed to support the breeder system. It would also be logical to enlarge the present electric power system (in preference to direct burning of fossil fuels), since the breeder economy will require a much bigger power-transmitting network than we have at present. And since the available uranium is insufficient to support expanded conventional nuclear power production for very long, many coal-burning power plants would be needed to supply the network with electricity until the breeder system is large enough to take over. As a result, coal would soon become the major bridging fuel, and coal production (which provides about 20 percent of the present energy budget) would expand considerably during transition.

Thus, once it is decided to undertake a transition to a renewable energy-producing system based on breeder reactors, that decision would dictate a series of sweeping changes in the present ways in which energy is produced and used. Even before breeders were introduced, production of uranium and coal would have to increase; the electric power that these fuels produce would replace the direct burning of oil and natural gas; devices that now use oil and natural gas—furnaces, stoves, cars, trucks, and railroads—would have to be replaced by electrically driven ones. There would have to be numerous, pervasive changes in industrial and agricultural production and transportation, which would add to the cost of building the new energy system itself.

A breeder-based energy system, as well as the transitional process that leads to it, would involve very grave environmental hazards. It is generally acknowledged that among the available sources of energy—oil, natural gas, coal, nuclear power, and solar energy—two involve by far the greatest environmental risks: coal and nuclear power. In the transition to a breeder system, the expanded scale of the mining and combustion of coal would considerably intensify the already serious environmental problems that these processes entail. One of the most important lessons of the accident at the Three Mile Island Nuclear Power Plant is that even after some twenty years of commercial use, conventional nuclear power remains an immature technology, subject to poorly understood and potentially catastrophic events. This is evident in the accounts of the accident. At a crucial point, when a decision about evacuating the people living in the area of the plant had to be made, Joseph M. Hendrie, chairman of the NRC, said that he and the Governor of Pennsylvania were operating ". . . almost totally in the blind. His [the Governor's] information is ambiguous; mine is nonexistent—I don't know—it's like a couple of blind men staggering around making decisions." Compared with conventional nuclear power plants like the one at Harrisburg, the breeder—a far more complex and much less tried technology—is in its infancy and is certain to be plagued for a long time by the failures, risks, and uncertainties that have brought conventional nuclear power to its present low state. Moreover, if breeders became a major source of power in the U.S., the amount of radioactive material that would have to be handled each year would rise sharply. Yet even now—some twenty years into the presumed nuclear age—we still lack an acceptable way to deal with the radioactive waste already on hand.

A breeder-based energy system threatens to poison the political atmosphere as well. Regardless of how a breeder is designed, the very size of the system would increase the risk that nuclear fuel might be stolen and fashioned into bombs. Breeders might use a plutonium fuel or a thorium/uranium 233 fuel. Although most of the discussion of the dangers of proliferation of nuclear weapons has thus far concentrated on plutonium breeders, the thorium/uranium 233 type seems to be nearly as dangerous. A recent comparison of how well the two fuel systems could be guarded against theft and proliferation gives the plutonium system a grade of B and the thorium-/uranium 233 system a grade of B+. On the usual four-point grade scale (B+ = 3.5, B = 3.0), this represents only a 17 percent difference between the dangers inherent in the two systems.

The Nuclear Regulatory Commission has been sufficiently concerned with these dangers to consider some of the implications of the measures needed to guard plutonium from potential thieves. A report on the legal consequences of these measures, prepared by Professor John H. Barton of the Stanford University Law School at the request of the commission, contains this chilling prediction:

Finally, dissidents might be seized and detained after a plutonium theft.... conceivably —although this interrogation issue has not been researched for this paper—detention could also be used as a step in a very troubling interrogation scheme—perhaps employing lie detectors or even torture. The normal deterrent to such practices—inadmissibility of evidence in court—would be ineffective under the conditions of a nuclear emergency.

In contrast to a breeder-based system, a solar system would deliver energy in a wide variety of forms. In forested areas, solar energy can be produced as a solid fuel (wood); in agricultural areas, as a liquid fuel (alcohol made from grain) or a gaseous fuel (methane made from manure or plant residues); in rainy, mountainous areas such as the Northwest, as hydroelectric power; in moderately or intensely sunny places, as photovoltaic electricity; in especially breezy places, as wind-generated electricity; almost everywhere, as direct heat. Thus the kinds and amounts of solar energy that can be produced depend very much on local conditions. In Minnesota, all the state's demand for energy (nearly three times as much, according to a recent survey) could be met by harvesting the cattail reeds that grow wild in most of that boggy state. (A recent report from Sweden, where there is a similar terrain and profusion of reeds, tells how they can be harvested for energy production without disrupting the marsh ecosystem.) In the Arizona desert, where harvesting the slow-growing cactus and tumbleweed for energy would yield little but ecological damage, the intense sunlight could readily be collected as heat, or in the form of electricity from photovoltaic cells. In the Dakota Badlands, where there is little vegetation and only moderate sunshine, there are strong winds, which can be used by windmills to generate electricity. There is, in sum, no solar panacea. No one solar process can efficiently produce energy in all parts of the country. A national solar-energy-gathering system needs to be as varied as the country itself, reflecting its uneven climate, terrain, and vegetation. Thus, in comparison with the breeder-based system—which produces only electricity—a solar system would produce energy in a multiplicity of forms, requiring considerably greater complexity in the overall design of the system.

A major complicating factor is that some places can produce more solar energy than is usable locally, while others need more energy than they can capture from the sun. A good example of the latter is a large and densely populated city such as New York. The city's sources of biomass are small, consisting only of sewage, garbage, and waste paper, which together might yield about 10 percent of the energy used in the city. Sunlight could be captured in solar collectors and photovoltaic cells, but because there are so many tall, closely packed buildings, the areas that might be used to hold these devices—rooftops, parking lots, and the southern sides of unshaded buildings—are rather limited. An example of the reverse situation is the forested area of upstate New York; its annual wood production represents more energy than the local activities need. It is evident, therefore, that a solar system must include a means of transporting energy from place to place in some suitable form.

The special property of solar energy—that it involves no economy of scale—greatly affects the strategy of energy transfer. Because there is no economy of scale, a small, local solar device will be just about as efficient as a large, distant one, and the cost, in energy and capital, of transmitting the energy from a central plant is then eliminated. If sufficient solar energy is available in a particular place to meet local needs, it makes sense to produce it and use it there.

In constructing a sensible solar energy system, all these factors must be woven together: Each of the several forms in which solar energy can be captured has to be produced in the regions where that particular form is most accessible. Each energy-using task must be supplied with energy in the form most suitable to it, in keeping with the simple requirements of weight and space and the more subtle imperatives of thermodynamics. And because solar devices have no economy of scale, energy required for local tasks should be produced locally wherever possible. Finally, when it is necessary to transmit energy, this should be done by whatever means best fits the economic and energetic design dictated by all these factors.

But these relationships are very abstract, and only delineate the design of a future, completed solar system—the Paradise which must somehow be reached from the present, earthly reality. To bring some reality into this abstract picture we must add the element of time. What steps, taken now, to alter the design of the *present* pattern of using nonrenewable fuels would effectively begin the transition toward the solar ideal? If we could answer this question we would have not only a plan of action directed toward a solar future, but also the kind of vision of that future that is essential to motivate such action. To answer this question we need a kind of mental motion picture that begins with a representation, or at least a sketch, of the present energy system (where different fuels are produced; how their energy is transported; how it is used) and is followed by a succession of patterns which change, with time, in a manner that efficiently, economically, and smoothly leads to a system in which all, or nearly all, the energy is derived—in various forms at different places—from the sun, and is distributed and used in ways that are compatible with that origin.

This is an intimidating task, but one that we must nevertheless confront. There is little experience, and certainly no ready-made blueprint, to guide us through such a complex problem, and any one effort to unscramble it is only that—a trial attempt with no more advance claim on the truth

than any other. My own approach is based on the notion of using a representation of the future solar energy system as a means of discovering its link to the real present. In this approach, one assembles the separate parts into a sketch of what an efficiently organized solar system would look like—once it is achieved. Then one examines this abstract system to seek out those elements in it that, although crucial to the structure of the overall system, are *not* in themselves solar and therefore could be put in place now. These non-solar elements would provide the bridge between the present, unsatisfactory reality and the still abstract, hoped-for future—thus depicting in real terms how the transition to solar energy might be accomplished.

The initial task of assembling a workable solar energy system is something like putting a jigsaw picture puzzle together. It is useful to begin with a few pieces that are obviously interrelated; then, as the visible fragment of the picture is enlarged, new relationships can be seen and new pieces fitted into it. Perhaps the easiest place to start is with the task for which there are no optional ways of providing energy: airplanes, which can operate only on liquid fuels. The easiest way to produce these fuels from sunlight is by way of biomass, yielding a fuel such as alcohol. At the present time airplane fuel accounts for only about 2 percent of the U.S. energy budget; land-based transportation that also uses liquid fuel now accounts for about 22 percent. While, for the reasons cited earlier, land transport is most efficiently driven by electricity, this conversion is likely to be difficult to achieve in every case. A solar liquid fuel, such as alcohol, will probably be needed to drive about a third of the land vehicles, especially high-powered tractors and construction machinery, and heavy trucks that carry freight not readily accommodated by railroads. Somewhere in the solar picture puzzle we must find a way of producing enough liquid fuel to operate all air transport and perhaps a third of ground transport.

However, wherever possible, land-based vehicles—railroads, urban mass transit, cars, and light trucks—ought to be driven by electricity, which will in any case be needed for stationary mechanical equipment, lighting, and communication. So the next piece in the puzzle that we must find is a suitable source of solar electricity to support these activities. Depending on the local situation, there are several options. First, to avoid the unnecessary cost of transmission, in both energy and capital, wherever the amount of available solar energy is sufficient, the electricity should be produced locally. If only electricity is needed—for example, for road or parking lot lighting—then it would make sense to produce it locally with photovoltaic cells (in relatively sunny places) or with windmills (in relatively windy places). However, in most places both heat and electricity will be needed. There—again assuming that the local intensity of sunshine is sufficient—solar collectors could be used to supply heat, and photovoltaic cells or windmills to provide electricity, thus avoiding the considerable inefficiencies of transmitting heat and electricity.

Where the local sources of solar energy are not sufficient to meet the local needs, as in a densely urbanized area, a different approach must be used: solar energy must be brought in from elsewhere. And to conform with the imperatives of the solar transition, the energy must be transmitted in a form, and used in a way, that maximizes efficiency. This brings us to a major segment of the solar picture: cogeneration, the local production of both useful heat and electricity from a combustible fuel. A cogenerator is an electric power plant that is so designed as to make use of the "waste" heat that a conventional plant ejects into the environment. For example, one recently designed cogenerator is simply a four-cylinder gasoline engine, ordinarily used to drive a Fiat automobile. The engine's drive shaft turns a generator that produces electricity; the engine's cooling system, which in the automobile gives off its heat into the environment by way of the radiator, is connected instead to a heat exchanger. This is a nest of interwoven pipes that transfers the heat produced by the engine to, let us say, a building's heating system. Thus the cogenerator produces energy in two useful forms—heat and electricity—which together can usually account for up to 90 percent of the energy originally contained in the fuel. In contrast, if the same engine were used to produce only electricity, with the heat wastefully ejected into the environment, its power output would represent, at most, 30 percent to 40 percent of the fuel's energy. Any engine that produces motion from a burning fuel can be used as a cogenerator: a gasoline or diesel engine, a gas turbine, or for that matter an old-fashioned steam engine. Installed in a residence, commercial building, or factory, a cogenerator can very efficiently heat it

in winter, cool it in summer, and throughout the year drive its electrically operated appliances. And since the cogenerator is sized to match the local need, capacity and demand are automatically tied together, so as to avoid the inefficiencies that occur whenever a large power plant is built to meet demand which increases in small, gradual steps. Because they can make very efficient use of liquid and gaseous fuels—which will be in relatively short supply in a solar system—cogenerators are a crucial part of such a system.

Here we come to the next part of the puzzle, for to take advantage of cogenerators we need to find a supply of solar fuel that is nonpolluting (so that it can be used in densely settled urban areas) and that can be transmitted efficiently (so that cogenerators can be used when the local supply of solar fuel is inadequate). For all the reasons cited earlier, solar methane is by far the best choice: It takes relatively little energy or capital to transmit it; it could be fed into the transmission line at numerous points, wherever the varied solar sources that can be converted to methane—sewage, garbage, manure, seaweed, crops—are available; it can readily be used to fuel a cogenerator driven by an internal combustion engine or a turbine; it can be burned anywhere without polluting the environment. Using methane in this way also fits nicely into those situations in which some local biomass is available, but in amounts that are too little or untimely to match the local demand. For example, at the height of the canning season, a cannery might produce more methane (from its waste) than is needed, and feed the surplus into the pipeline. At other times, when the local supply is short, the cannery might draw methane from the pipeline.

Now, with a pipeline for widespread collection and distribution of solar methane in place, we can see how to fit another major feature into the solar picture. This concerns the possibility of collecting electric power from photovoltaic cells and windmills, produced in places where it is readily available in excess of local needs, in order to bolster the total national energy supply. The energy will have to be transmitted over considerable distances, but for the reasons already cited, that can be done more efficiently if the electricity is first converted to gas. This can be accomplished by using the electricity to produce hydrogen gas (from water), which can then be readily converted to methane, chemically or through the action of certain microorganisms. Alternatively, the hydrogen can simply be added to the methane pipeline. (Mixtures containing 10 percent to 20 percent hydrogen can be piped and used in equipment designed for pure methane.) In this way, wherever electricity can be produced in excess of local needs, it can be shipped to more needy places in the form of a gaseous fuel, and there converted into electricity and heat by a cogenerator, or into electricity alone by a fuel cell. (A fuel cell is a device that, supplied with oxygen and a gaseous fuel such as hydrogen or methane, very efficiently produces electricity.)

The environment also forms a vital part of this solar picture. Fortunately, the solar devices that make economic sense are also quite compatible with the environment. Solar collectors, photovoltaic cells, and windmills simply transfer solar heat from one place to another. Their effects would be unnoticeable in the heat-transfer processes which occur naturally in the changes of the weather. The production of fuels from biomass fits nicely into the natural ecological cycles that support agriculture, and when burned, these fuels (or hydrogen produced from solar electricity) produce only water and carbon dioxide. And since the carbon dioxide produced when a solar fuel burns is exactly equal to the amount absorbed, photosynthetically, when the fuel is produced, this process does not contribute to the untoward environmental effects of rising levels of carbon dioxide in the atmosphere. Unlike the present high-tension power lines which disrupt the landscape, methane pipelines would be underground—where, unfortunately, they would be subject, as are the present natural gas pipelines, to fires and explosions.

A final piece of the solar picture puzzle concerns storage. Since the availability of solar energy depends on the natural cycles that govern the planet's behavior—the alternation of day and night, the seasonal changes in solar intensity, changes in cloud cover—there are times when energy is needed but is not immediately available. Storage is therefore essential. There are well-known devices capable of storing the different forms of solar energy in the amounts required to meet local short-term needs: tanks of hot water, bins of grain and other forms of biomass, rechargeable batteries, tanks of liquid fuels or of pressurized hydrogen or methane. However, a national solar system also requires storage on a na-

tional scale—a fact that is usually overlooked by both the proponents and the opponents of solar energy. The annual output of a wholly solar national energy system would depend on the weather, and if the system was just large enough to meet the national demand in a relatively sunny year, it might fail disastrously in a particularly cold or cloudy year. One can, of course, deal with this problem by building a solar system large enough to operate effectively in the worst conceivable annual weather. But this would incur a large added cost that would be unnecessary in most years. The more efficient way to deal with the problem is the ancient one that has been traditional in our oldest solar enterprise, farming: grain overproduced in good years is stored in preparation for bad years. The same thing could be done by storing energy on a national scale. But again, methane is the only form of energy that could be handled in this way. (Constructing tanks and bins large enough for a national store of liquid fuel, or biomass, would be prohibitively expensive.) With a national methane pipeline system in place, in good years excess methane could be produced and then pumped for storage (perhaps mixed with some hydrogen) into the underground formations that once held natural gas, many of which will then, of course, be empty. The same strategy could be used to compensate for the seasonal imbalance between energy production (which is likely to be highest in the summer) and energy demand (which is likely to be highest in the winter).

It is tempting to further refine this solar sketch, but that would be likely to give it only a patina of dubious detail. The detailed way in which energy is produced and used in a solar system is necessarily determined by local conditions, and generalizations are likely only to blur the elegant fit between source and task that is essential to its efficiency. Consider, for example, the different ways of using solar energy for a particular purpose, let us say to operate a stadium's floodlights. Since the stadium needs little or no heat, it would be inefficient to use a methane-driven cogenerator to produce the electricity—unless the stadium happened to be near a housing development or shopping center that needed the heat. If the stadium was in a sufficiently sunny area, it could be equipped with a photovoltaic cell/battery system designed to collect enough power during the day to supply the lights at night. How the system was designed (and what it would cost) would depend on how much sunshine was expected during an average day, and how often the stadium would need nighttime illumination. On the other hand, if the stadium was close to a methane pipeline, it might be better to equip it with a set of fuel cells. Finally, when the costs of alternative schemes had been worked out, it might be discovered that a cogeneration scheme would produce enough savings to tip the economic scales in favor of roofing the stadium and using the cogenerators' heat to warm it in winter and cool it in summer. This example warns us to forgo the fascination of devising detailed solar plans at a distance. To be efficient—as it must—the production and use of solar energy need to be integrated into the design and purposes of the activity it supports. And this can be done only on the scene, where there is an intimate appreciation of the relevant physical, operational, and economic problems.

Failure to appreciate the importance of such integration can readily lead to undue pessimism about solar energy. For example, solar schemes for processes such as grain-drying, in which warm air is used, are sometimes criticized because they appear to require expensive heat-storage devices. However, a solar grain-drying system developed at Purdue University has solved this problem in a way that teaches us something about the importance of integration. The grain itself is used to store the heat. Solar-heated air is blown up through a bin of grain during the day; some of the heat remains in the lower levels of grain so that, during the night, it can warm unheated air and continue the drying process. Here the need for a new, costly storage device is avoided by a careful integration of the solar system into the existing farm operations. Similarly, a photovoltaic cell system (which requires batteries) can be more economic if it is integrated into the operation of a household that uses an electric car (in which batteries are essential) or of a factory that uses battery-operated hand tools.

On a larger scale, the principle of integration may require that some industrial operations be relocated in order to give them access to ample sources of solar energy. This may be particularly important in the case of steel mills and other primary metal industries, which are necessarily large and very demanding of energy. Ideally, such industries should be located near the largest sources of solar energy—hydroelectric plants—

which, in a national solar system, will probably have to be reserved for such uses.

But once again, the importance of integrating solar energy into the detailed design of the production process it must support reminds us that this cannot be done at a distance. The production and use of solar energy is, necessarily, a subsidiary part of a particular productive activity and must be designed to serve it. A sensible solar system cannot be created from a detailed, central plan. It cannot be designed from the top down, but must emerge from the necessarily local decisions that can determine whether a stadium should be roofed in; whether a family should buy an electric car; or whether a factory should replace cord-operated power hand tools with battery-operated ones.

Rough as it is, this sketch of what a solar system —once completed—might look like does delineate two predominant features that link this future abstraction to present reality. One of these links is the pervasive, integrating role that a particular form of energy, methane (or a methane/hydrogen mixture), would play in the system: as a means of collecting solar energy from local points of production and transmitting it to local points of use; as an environmentally benign fuel capable of efficiently yielding heat or electricity alone, or heat and electricity together; as a uniquely effective means of providing a long-term, national store of energy to compensate for seasonal and annual fluctuations in supply and demand. The second link is the local cogeneration of heat and electricity, which is the key to the joint, efficient, widespread production of these forms of energy from solar sources. Together these two features can build the sought-for bridge between the non-renewable present and the solar future, for they are not only crucial elements of the renewable solar system, but are existing, easily expanded components of the present *non*renewable energy system.

Methane, a renewable solar fuel, is completely interchangeable with a present nonrenewable fuel, natural gas, for the main burnable constituent of natural gas is, in fact, simply methane. What is more, a good deal of the needed gas distribution system is already in place to carry natural gas. In the transition, solar methane gradually could replace natural gas without disrupting the production processes that now depend on this fuel. This could be done by building methane-generating plants wherever a suitable source of biomass is readily available—garbage and sewage in cities; crops, manure, agricultural residues, and cannery wastes in farming areas; wood in forest areas; seaweed along the coast. As they are built, these plants gradually could take over the task of feeding fuel into the pipelines that already supply natural gas to factories, homes, and commercial establishments. There need be no interruption in supplies, no "shortages"; only a gradual shutting down of the flow of increasingly expensive natural gas from existing wells, and a gradual rise in the flow of solar methane. Such a transition would be relatively inexpensive, for it would make good use of the existing pipelines, the cost of which would otherwise be written off as natural gas escalated in price and its use declined. No furnaces or stoves would need to be replaced. The inflationary impact of energy prices would be tempered, for as the transition progressed, the price of the mixed natural gas/solar methane fuel would be increasingly governed by the stable cost of solar methane, rather than by the exponentially rising cost of natural gas.

Such a transition could be so smooth, gradual, and unspectacular that it might hardly be noticed. Indeed, it has already begun, quite unnoticed, in Chicago. In 1978 the Peoples Gas Company of Chicago began to buy methane generated from manure obtained from several cattle feed lots in Guymon, Oklahoma. Each day about 1.6 million cubic feet of methane is pumped into the pipeline that carries natural gas from Oklahoma to Chicago. It is sold to the utility at $1.95 per thousand cubic feet (the gas deregulation bill brings the 1979 price of new natural gas to about $2.08 per thousand cubic feet). Additional income is obtained from the residue, which is sold as feed or fertilizer. Thus every pot of water on a gas-burning stove in Chicago is now heated in part—thus far, a very small part—by renewable, solar energy. However limited in scale, this is concrete evidence that natural gas is, indeed, a solar-bridging fuel; that the solar transition is not only possible but real.

The second crucial factor in a solar energy system—methane-fueled, local cogeneration of heat and electricity—sounds like an inventor's utopian dream: It conserves energy and capital; it reduces energy costs; it eliminates environmental pollu-

tion. But it is, in fact, already in use. According to a recent British book on cogenerators, which "is believed to be the first comprehensive textbook in this new field," in 1967 there were some five hundred successful cogeneration systems in the U.S., many of them operating on natural gas. Among the installations that are described in some detail in the textbook are the following. In New York City, two good-size gas-fired cogeneration systems have been installed by the Brooklyn Union Gas Company. One, at Rochdale Village in Queens, serves a 170-acre complex consisting of twenty 14-story apartment buildings (a total of 5,840 apartments) and two shopping centers. The only energy that enters the complex is natural gas; there is no connection to the electric utility. The gas fires steam boilers, which feed high-pressure steam into turbines that drive electric generators. The "waste" low-pressure steam heats the buildings in the winter and air-conditions them in the summer, and supplies them with hot water throughout the year. A similar system provides energy for the Warbasse housing complex in Coney Island. In Little Rock, Arkansas, the Park Plaza shopping center, with 240,000 square feet of floor space, obtains all its energy from a gas-fueled cogenerator, as do the Student Hostel at Ohio State University (two 24-story buildings) in Columbus, Ohio, a hay-drying plant at St. Cloud, Florida, and a series of apartment complexes (a total of some 1,000 units) in Kansas City, Missouri. Such schemes yield considerable savings in money and energy. For example, the natural-gas-fired cogenerator at the Hillcrest Junior High School in Edmonton, Alberta, uses 20 percent less energy to provide the needed heat and electricity than a conventional system. The cogenerator costs about $50,000 more than conventional equipment, but the school saved about $9,300 in fuel and power costs in the first year of operation, so that the extra cost would be recovered in about five or six years.

With a gas-fired cogenerator in place, establishments such as Rochdale Village would be in an excellent position to hold their energy costs down, despite the rising price of natural gas—if solar methane were available. Suppose, for example, New York City, the state, or the federal government constructed a plant to convert New York City garbage and sewage (or perhaps the huge underwater dump of sewage sludge that lies off the Long Island coast) into methane. Such a project is an immediate technical practicality. (Indeed, the city's existing sewage treatment plants already produce methane, although inefficiently, as a by-product. The Starrett City housing development in Brooklyn is investigating the possibility of using methane from a nearby sewage plant in its cogeneration system.) Based on the expected cost of producing methane from sewage and the rise in the price of natural gas mandated by the recent deregulation legislation, if the complex supplemented its fuel with solar methane it would be saving money on its fuel costs in the near future. And the savings would increase year by year as the price of natural gas continues its unending escalation while the cost of renewable solar methane remains constant. We will, after all, never run out of garbage and sewage and their price will not escalate.

Meanwhile the New York area would reap other benefits. Conversion of garbage, sewage, and underwater sludge to methane would rid the environment of major pollutants. The organic residue from methane production is an excellent fertilizer; used on Long Island farms instead of inorganic nitrogen, the residue would help reduce the pollution of surface waters due to nitrate leaching from fields now heavily fertilized with inorganic nitrogen. Solar energy could be introduced, and all these advantages realized, now, without waiting for a research "breakthrough" or for residents to develop a life style suitable to the arrival of what the Department of Energy likes to call an "exotic" energy source. Indeed, they would hardly know it had arrived, unless some slight difference in the burning qualities of the solar methane and the natural gas which it replaced required an adjustment in the kitchen stove pilot lights. In Rochdale Village or Starrett City—or wherever energy needs are met by natural-gas-fired cogenerators—the solar transition could start tomorrow.

At least one operator of a large office building in Manhattan is hoping to switch from conventional energy sources to cogeneration. But the plan has been blocked thus far because the proposed cogenerators would use diesel fuel, and thereby contribute to the already considerable level of air pollution in the city. The use of natural gas would get around that problem. Until recently, cogeneration was thought of only in connection with large buildings or complexes, since only large-size equipment has been available. Now the Fiat company of Italy has brought cogeneration down to the scale of a single-family house, by introducing the small cogenerator (TOTEM) based on its four-cylinder automobile engine. The unit will run on gasoline, methane, natural gas, or alcohol. It can convert 66 percent of the fuel's energy into heat and 26 percent into electricity; only 8 percent is lost. (A conventional home furnace will convert only 40 percent to 65 percent of the fuel's energy to space heat.) For producing electricity alone, the TOTEM unit is almost as efficient as a central electric generating station; but whereas the heat lost at the central power station is wasted, the cogenerator's heat is used. The TOTEM unit costs about $6,000, or about $400 per kilowatt of electric capacity. This compares well with the capital cost of central power stations, which is $500 to $1,500 per kilowatt of capacity.

With such small units available, the solar transition could be brought to those residents of New York who need it most—the poor. It is a notorious fact that in large areas of the city where poor families live—for example, the southern sections of the Bronx and the East New York area of Brooklyn—housing has become shamefully deteriorated. Most of the homes that still stand need new heating systems, and the many burned-out homes need to be rebuilt. This is an opportunity to install small gas-fired cogenerators, affording immediate savings in utility costs and later—as supplies of solar methane are produced in sufficient amount—freedom from the yearly increase in utility costs, which now take such a large part of a poor family's budget. In rebuilding these areas it might be even more economical to install a small power plant, equipped with cogenerators, that would supply all the neighborhood houses with electricity, heat, and air conditioning—and for that matter with new jobs—besides giving the community a vitalizing sense of independence.

Once a gas-fired cogenerator is in place, it does more than save the consumer money and the nation energy. Such a cogenerator system is also ready to accept three different forms of solar energy. First, the natural gas it uses could be replaced gradually by solar methane. Then, solar collectors could readily be added to the system, to produce heat for space heat and hot water (and with more advanced collectors, for air conditioning as well). With the cogenerator system already in place and capable of providing heat during the worst part of winter, the solar system could be kept to a size that maximizes its economic advantage. Finally, a building or neighborhood energy system already equipped with a cogenerator and its own electric system would be admirably prepared to add photovoltaic cells, with no further costs for the necessary power control equipment. With the addition of collectors and photovoltaic cells, the amount of gas used for cogeneration could be cut back. In the early stages of a solar transition, this would reduce the use of natural gas, thereby freeing the consumer from the effects of its escalating price. In the later stages of the transition, when most of the gas in the pipeline would be solar methane, local production of heat and electricity from solar collectors and photovoltaic cells would save the gas for situations in which local energy sources are insufficient.

Here, then, is a practical picture of at least one part of the solar transition. It would proceed by a series of linked steps. First, natural-gas-fired cogenerators are installed; then, as increasing numbers of methane plants are built, pipeline solar methane gradually replaces the natural gas; and as heat from solar collectors and electricity from photovoltaic cells (and in some places, from windmills) become more plentiful, these sources replace some of the pipeline gas. Beginning with the cogenerator—an existing, practical, *non-solar* device which saves the consumer money and the nation nonrenewable energy—the transition proceeds, each step facilitating the next, until the entire need for energy is fully met by renewable, thrifty solar sources. In this way, the seemingly abstract solar future can be reached from a start firmly anchored in the present reality.

Thus rooted in the real present; able to envision, at least in part, the solar future; and knowing the links that connect the two, we are enabled now to discern how the nation might negotiate the historic passage to solar energy. It is generally agreed that if it can be done, replacing all, or nearly all (90 percent to 95 percent, perhaps), of our present nonrenewable energy sources with solar energy might take fifty years or so. If the present patterns of energy use were maintained, the total demand for energy might double in that time. However, if we made the necessary effort to conserve energy where the waste is greatest—for example, through the widespread use of cogenerators and electrified mass transit—it should be possible to keep the increase down to about one-

third of the present demand. The task of the transition, then, is to increase gradually the total amount of energy consumed from its present (1977) value of 76 quads to about 100 quads in 2027, and simultaneously replace the present nonrenewable energy sources (imported and domestic oil, nuclear power, coal, and natural gas) with solar sources. Keeping in mind the decisive roles that natural gas (as the bridging fuel) and cogeneration (as an energy-efficient prelude to the entry of solar energy) must play in the transition, we can begin to see the pattern it might follow.

In the initial phase of the transition, in order to meet the rising demand for heat and electricity, natural gas–fired cogenerators would be installed wherever possible and more extensive gas distribution systems built to supply them. At the same time, wherever feasible, present installations that use electricity for heating would also be replaced by gas-fired cogenerators. While these measures will increase the overall efficiency of the national energy system, the fuels saved will necessarily be those that are used for power production: coal, uranium, and to a lesser extent, oil. This means that the increased overall demand for energy will have to be met by a gradual expansion of the use of natural gas, probably from its present annual figure of 20 quads to about 35 quads in the twenty-fifth year after the transition begins.

Meanwhile, during the first twenty-five years of the transition, the production of solar energy would slowly increase. Starting now, wherever feasible, solar collectors would be installed to provide heat; alcohol produced from waste and crops would begin to replace gasoline; methane, produced wherever there is enough suitable biomass, would be fed into the expanding pipeline system that already carries natural gas. In five years or so after the start of the transition, the use of photovoltaic cells and wind generators would begin to expand appreciably. Gradually, the total production of solar energy would increase until it amounted to perhaps 20 percent of the total energy budget by the twenty-fifth year. At that point, halfway through the transition, solar energy and expanded natural gas production would account for somewhat over half the total energy budget. With these additions to the national energy supply, it would be possible, for example, to eliminate all oil imports over the first twenty-five year period of the transition without increasing the present rate of producing domestic oil, coal, and nuclear power. Alternatively, a particularly useful way to launch the solar transition would be to use it, initially, to replace nuclear power. One of the unfortunate consequences of the recent accident at the Three Mile Island Nuclear Power Plant is that it has confronted areas—such as Chicago and New England—especially dependent on nuclear power with a painful dilemma. Residents of those areas now know that they too face the uncertainties, disruption, and potential catastrophe that confronted the people in the Harrisburg area last March. But they also know that their supply of energy cannot be cut back without courting economic disaster. The solar transition could help relieve the distress of these regions, which are now hostage to the anxieties of their proximity to nuclear power plants. The energy-saving and energy-producing measures of the solar transition that are ready for use—for example, solar collectors, natural gas–driven cogenerators, and photovoltaic cells—could be introduced at once, allowing these areas gradually to close down nuclear plants without disrupting their essential supply of energy. In effect, in the first half of the transition, the increased use of both natural gas and solar energy could replace imported oil or nuclear power, and accommodate the expected increase in the overall demand for energy.

In the next twenty-five years, as solar sources continued to expand (especially the more novel ones, such as hydrogen production), it would be possible to reduce gradually to zero the production of domestic oil, coal, and nuclear power, while natural gas production fell to 10 quads per year (about half its present rate). At that point the system would be about 90 percent solar. Thereafter, the 10 percent contribution of natural gas gradually could be eliminated, but it would be important to retain this source as a stand-by to compensate for seasonal and annual changes in climate.

To carry us through the transition, this scheme would require the production of a total of 1,350 quads of the bridging fuel, natural gas, over the fifty-year period. Is that much natural gas available in the United States? It is commonly agreed that the geological formations that are now being tapped for natural gas in the U.S. contain about 900 to 1,300 quads of produceable fuel, somewhat short of enough to support the transition. However, evidence developed in the last few years has drastically changed this outlook—for the better. It now appears that there are much larger sources of natural gas in the U.S. than the conventional ones. These "unconventional" sources of natural gas have been encountered repeatedly over the years, during exploration of conventional oil and gas formations, but they have been largely neglected thus far. One such unconventional source is "geopressurized methane," which occurs in a hot briny solution, at depths of 8,000 to 15,000 feet, especially along the Texas coast. Another unconventional source is natural gas held in tight geological formations. In Appalachia, thousands of wells have produced natural gas from these formations, but flow rates are low and they are of limited use. Now, however, a fairly simple way has been found to break up the tight shale formation that inhibits the flow of gas. A mixture of water and tiny particles of sand (or other material) is pumped into the well under high pressure. The pressure breaks up the formation and forces the particles into the crevices that are opened up. When the pressure is released, the particles keep the crevices open, allowing gas to flow freely. The same technique is being used to release natural gas from tight sand formations in the Southwest.

In August 1978, at a meeting of gas industry experts in Aspen, Colorado, it was agreed that these unconventional sources in the United States might amount to a total of 5,000 to 10,000 quads. Earlier reports gave similar figures and estimated the potential U.S. sources of natural gas (about 87 percent "unconventional") at about 7,000 quads. According to the industry experts, these new sources of natural gas can probably be produced at a cost of about $2 to $3 per thousand cubic feet. This is about the cost that conventional natural gas production is expected to reach within a few years. Thus there does seem to be enough natural gas available—at a price that is reasonable, compared to the alternative, imported oil—to support the transition. After the transition is complete, the natural gas supply is also sufficient to serve as a stand-by for many years, or until solar methane and hydrogen is sufficiently plentiful to produce a surplus, for storage.

This brings us to the second practical question: Could the country eventually produce enough solar energy to meet the total national demand? In theory, the answer is yes, for the total amount of solar energy that falls on the land is hundreds of times larger than we need. But a practical answer is more difficult, for this requires that sufficient solar energy be produced in the appropriate forms. Producing enough heat from solar collectors, or electricity from photovoltaic cells, is only a matter of extending these devices over a sufficient area. The present demand for heat could be met by solar collectors covering about 0.44 percent of the U.S. land area, and the demand for electricity could be met by using another 0.12 percent for photovoltaic cells (operating with the efficiency of presently available cells, about 10 percent). Given that streets and roads take up about one percent of the land area, this is not an insuperable problem.

By prudently using available organic wastes, developing new sources such as seaweeds, and—most important—judiciously reorganizing agriculture so that it yields, efficiently, *both* food and solar fuels, the country could meet its crucial need for liquid and gaseous fuels. The alcohol available from agriculture could certainly provide for the expected needs of aviation (about 1.3 quads), with enough left over to fuel heavy land-based vehicles that are not readily operated electrically. The 20 quads of methane and hydrogen that could be produced, divided about equally between industry and the residential/commercial sector, could take care of the demand for heat and electricity not readily met by local solar collectors, photovoltaic cells, and windmills.

In sum, the route to a solar future is open.

The choice of which route the nation ought to follow in the transition from the present, increasingly intolerable reliance on nonrenewable energy to a renewable energy system now lies before us. Both of the optional routes are technically possible. Several apparently successful breeder reactors have been built in Europe, and although they do not seem to regenerate fuel very efficiently as yet, there is no reason to doubt that they could, in theory, provide us with the needed energy for a number of centuries. And as we have seen, properly organized around the use of natural gas as a bridging fuel, a transition to a national solar energy system is also possible. Both routes would be costly and both would affect much more in the nation's life than the production of energy.

Adopting the breeder-based nuclear power route involves a number of very grave questions. These include: the growing uncertainties about the safety of nuclear power plants; whether radio-active wastes can be safely stored, and if so, how; how to meet the heavy demand for increasingly costly capital for building nuclear power plants; how to cope with the resultant escalation of utility rates; what can be done about the terrifying prospects of nuclear proliferation and radioactive contamination inherent in the extensive traffic in plutonium, thorium, or uranium 233 that would be inevitable in a breeder-based power system.

The solar choice raises equally difficult, but different, questions. Some of them are: whether the oil and gas industry is able—or willing—to produce more natural gas from the known reserves and to expand gas pipelines at a reasonable cost; whether industry, the auto industry for example, is willing to invest in the large-scale production of cogenerators; how to provide the loans that consumers need to invest in collectors and other solar equipment; whether the federal government (or for that matter states and cities) would be willing to buy sufficient photovoltaic cells so that production can be expanded and the price reduced to the point of invading the conventional electric market; whether the petroleum industry will tolerate the competition from farmers' production of solar fuels and the utility industry the competition from locally produced electricity.

The social and political consequences of the choice are immense. Breeder reactors, and the intense use of coal that must precede them, would intensify greatly our present, already serious, environmental problems. The breeder route would concentrate most of the nation's energy system in the hands of either the very largest corporations or the federal government—the only institutions capable of meeting the huge cost of even a single breeder. The need to protect the system would probably bring it under the control of the military and, according to Professor John Barton, could lead to grave threats to the legal processes that protect personal and political freedom in the U.S.

In contrast, solar energy is completely compatible with the environment. (The sun's nuclear reactions are safely contained within it, 93 million miles away; its ultraviolet radiation is largely absorbed by the earth's ozone layer; the physical impact of using solar energy is lost in the variations of the weather.) Sunshine is widely distributed and is best exploited by decentralized operations, rather than by a few huge centralized plants controlled by supercorporations under military protection. Solar energy is inherently benign, and when a pump fails in a solar device there is no need to call upon the President to visit the scene in order to calm the fear of catastrophe. No form of solar energy can be turned into a huge bomb; no political fantasist or power-hungry dictator could use solar energy as an instrument of terror; no one need be tortured to recover a stolen solar device.

Is it necessary to choose *between* the two routes? Can we not follow both of them, emphasizing the advantages and minimizing the hazards of each? Unfortunately, we cannot; the two routes are inherently, intractably, incompatible. The breeder-based system would require the creation of a huge electrical transmission network and the adaptation of all energy-using tasks to this single source. In a solar system, methane/hydrogen pipelines eventually would take the place of most of the electrical network, and energy would be produced, in a variety of forms, in relatively small, local units. The cost of either system would be so great that the nation simply could not afford to build both of them. We can take one route or the other, not both.

It is evident, then, that a choice must be made between the two routes toward a renewable national energy system; that the choice must be made now; and that it involves very grave and portentous decisions about the nation's economic, social, and political future. Although these issues clearly should have been considered in the debates on the National Energy Plan, they were not. At their best, the debates were tangential to the real issues; at their worst, they served to confuse them. The administration's position on the breeder has been particularly troublesome. When, two weeks before the National Energy Plan was due, Mr. Carter announced that he wanted to end the Clinch River (plutonium) breeder project, environmentalists were jubilant. They knew that without the breeder it made little sense to continue the conventional nuclear power program, for the uranium supplies would run out. But once again, the administration's energy policy was not quite what it seemed, for tucked away on page 70 of *The National Energy Plan* is the statement that "the President is proposing to reduce the funding for the existing [plutonium] breeder program and to *redirect it toward the evaluation of alternative breeders, advanced converter reactors and other fuel cycles*" [emphasis

added]. Thus the National Energy Plan not only proposed a sharp increase in the construction of conventional nuclear reactors; it also envisaged that they would be followed by a system of nuclear breeders. Despite campaign claims that nuclear power would be used only as a "last resort," the administration has been, in fact, strongly committed to both a nuclear present and a nuclear future. However, when the full impact of the incident at Harrisburg is felt, they may find it expedient to change this policy. At the same time, the Plan played down the development of solar energy; according to the Plan, solar energy would account for only 1.6 percent of the increment in demand between 1976 and 1985, a figure that Dr. Schlesinger later reduced to one percent. Administration spokesmen have recently reinforced this position. Thus John O'Leary, Deputy Secretary of Energy, told a meeting of the American Public Power Association in October 1978 that "there is no place for solar energy in this century . . . we can have two options—coal and nuclear power."

If there was any question about where Mr. Carter stands on the importance of developing solar energy, he made this quite clear on November 6, 1978, when he signed the Solar Photovoltaic Energy Research, Development and Demonstration Act of 1978. Among other things, this bill authorized the government to make a substantial purchase of photovoltaic cells—the step that the FEA Task Force had shown would lead to the rapid commercialization of this device. However, when Mr. Carter signed the bill he refused to authorize the purchase:

It is still too early to concentrate on commercialization of photovoltaics. Photovoltaic systems hold great promise; but in the short run we must emphasize research and development, including fundamental work on the physical properties of these systems, so that this promise can be realized. Therefore I will not propose to the Congress that a broad Federal solar photovoltaic purchase program tied to the specific goals of this Act be undertaken soon.

And since then, in the aftermath of the accident at Harrisburg, Mr. Carter has reiterated his view that we must continue to develop nuclear power. Now that it has become clear that the administration is committed to the development of a breeder reactor, the large role allotted to nuclear power, to coal, and to electricity generally in the Plan falls into place. With coal relied on heavily as the bridging fuel, the nation's centralized power network would need to be considerably expanded. Consequently, should the Plan be carried out, by 1985 the entire national energy system would become heavily dependent on centralized electric power production. A considerable part of the national power output would be produced by conventional nuclear power plants, so that when, by the turn of the century, it became clear that nuclear fuel was running out, a serious shortage of electricity would be threatened. At that point, with the energy system so dependent on it, there would be no choice but to extend the life of the nuclear power system by introducing the breeder, whether plutonium based or the thorium breeder that Mr. Carter seems to prefer. Here, then, is the transition to renewable energy inherent in the design of the National Energy Plan, and in administration policy.

This helps to explain why the debate on the National Energy Plan was so irrelevant to the problem of solving the energy crisis. The Plan seemed to be based on a perception of the crisis that was at once misleading and covert. On one level the Plan was put forward as a conservation program—an effort to cut the use of energy in order to stave off the day of reckoning when we will supposedly "run out of oil." On this level the Plan was misleading; it was not designed to solve the energy crisis—which requires a transition to renewable energy—but merely to delay it. All Mr. Carter's exhortations were linked to the conservation proposals; this was the loudly publicized face of the Plan.

But hidden behind the Plan's intricate manipulations and discussed by neither the administration nor the Congress is its deeper thrust. On this level the Plan seems to reflect a much clearer understanding that the energy crisis springs from the nonrenewability of our present sources and that the only way to solve it—as distinct from delaying it—is to carry out a transition to renewable sources of energy. With little fanfare, the Plan sets in motion just such a transition—to the renewable source of energy represented by a vast nuclear power system based on breeder-regenerated fuel. This, the unpublicized part of the Plan, would commit the nation, unwittingly, to a vision of the future that is anathema to many Americans.

It is now apparent that the United States does not yet have an energy policy explicitly designed to solve the energy crisis; nor have the momentous issues involved in establishing such a policy been subjected to legislative debate and public judgment. But we now know how to remedy this defect. To solve the energy crisis we must establish a national policy for the transition from the present, nonrenewable energy system to a renewable one. To create such a policy in keeping with the principles of democratic governance, we need to compare, in public debate, how the two possible sources of renewable energy—breeder-based nuclear power and solar energy—will affect the national welfare, and then choose between them.

7

THE HISTORIC PASSAGE:
The Politics of Energy

Despite the confusion that has surrounded the effort to cope with the energy crisis, clarity has been forced on us by events. Originally, Mr. Carter claimed that we are "running out" of oil and natural gas, and cannot acquire these fuels any faster. Now we have learned that the United States has huge "unconventional" deposits of natural gas many times larger than conventional ones, and that Mexico has oil reserves nearly as large as Saudi Arabia's—much more than enough to support a transition to solar energy. As late as November 1978, the administration asserted that promoting conservation by raising the price of energy would not aggravate inflation. Now this claim has been nullified, for in December the White House itself denounced OPEC's decision to raise the price of oil by 14.5 percent in 1979 (about the same increase that the gas deregulation bill is likely to cause in that year), because "This large price hike will impede the programs to maintain world economic recovery and to reduce inflation." The National Energy Plan strongly favored nuclear power over solar energy. Now the pervasive force that the administration relies on to guide the economy—the free market—has delivered the opposite verdict: in 1979, while the nuclear power industry—already in an economic decline—staggers under the impact of the accident at Harrisburg, farmers in the Midwest are investing their entrepreneurial ingenuity—not to speak of millions of their dollars—in the production of a solar fuel, grain alcohol.

Thus, while the administration has been nudging us in one direction, the realities of the world have moved, more forcefully, in another. Mr. Carter said that the effort to develop a national energy policy would test his political leadership. He has failed the test, and after two years of confusion we are back where we started from: the United States still needs an energy policy. If this judgment seems harsh, it is nevertheless supported by the administration's recent action, or rather inaction, on energy. In January 1979, three months after the passage of the National Energy Act, Mr. Carter delivered his State of the Union message. If the act had indeed created a new national program to deal with the energy crisis, one would have expected Mr. Carter to take considerable notice of its impact on the state of the union in his address. Instead, he devoted less than a dozen words to the subject, prompting the Senate majority whip, Robert Byrd, who had faithfully pushed the administration's bill through the Senate, to ask: "Has energy suddenly become a stepchild?"

If this is the melancholy outcome of the effort to create an energy policy, the more cheerful news is that we now know how it can be done. We now know that the energy crisis is the inescapable result of our nearly total dependence on nonrenewable sources—which, as they rise in price, place an intolerable burden on the economy; that only a transition to a renewable energy source—solar energy or the nuclear breeder—can solve this problem; that the choice between these two options involves grave economic, social, and political issues, which need to be resolved in a national debate; that despite the administration's fumbling, the relevant facts are in hand and are ready to be put before the American people for decision.

"The American people" is not a uniform body, but a collection of groups that occupy different, and in some respects conflicting, positions in the economic system, which may be best served by different energy policies. Prominent among these groups are consumers, farmers, labor, the entrepreneurs and managers of the industries that use energy, the entrepreneurs and managers of the industries that produce and distribute energy. Each group needs to examine for itself how the choice between the two alternative routes toward a national system of renewable energy—or for that matter, if they wish, neither—would meet its own interests. Then the legislative forum which is supposed to perform that function—the Congress—can consider what plan of action would yield the greatest benefit to the greatest number.

In order to understand how each of the different economic groups would be affected by the optional energy policies, we need to consider the basic role that energy plays in the economy. It is helpful to start with the end result, or purpose, of the economic system and then work backward to discover how that purpose depends on energy. It is generally agreed that the aim of all economic activity is to help meet human needs by producing the desired goods and services, such as the goods produced by farms and factories or the services produced by hospitals, telephone systems, banks, and movie theaters. In the aggregate, these goods and services are the output of the system of production. In turn, every production process requires the expenditure of energy—to drive the farm's tractors and the factory's assembly lines; to heat the hospital and light its operating rooms; to power the telephones and the repairmen's trucks; to run the bank's computers and the theater's movie projectors. The value to society of the energy that is expended in running the production system depends on the amount of goods and services that it helps to produce—or the *use-value* that the energy generates.

The efficiency with which energy generates such use-value depends in part on thermodynamics: how much useful work is gotten out of each unit of energy and is applied to the production process. Thus a cogenerator will extract more useful, productive work (in the form of heat and electricity) from a given amount of fuel than a power plant (which produces only electricity). The efficiency with which energy serves the purpose of the economic system also depends on an economic factor: the cost of the machinery, labor, and other economic resources that are used in order to produce and distribute the energy. A cogenerator may cost one-fourth the price of a power plant of the same capacity, and therefore consume that much less capital. On the other hand, it takes less labor to maintain and repair the power plant than the thousands of cogenera-

tors needed to yield the same amount of energy.

Whether the renewable system is breeder-based or solar, it will largely *replace* the existing energy-producing system. Economists think of the cost of replacing the economic system's productive machinery as a maintenance cost. All machinery wears out in time (in the jargon of economics, it depreciates), and unless it is replaced by new machines of equal productive capacity, economic output will decrease. In general, the economic resources (raw materials, energy, labor, and capital) that are needed to replace a particular sector of the economy, such as the energy system, simply maintain the economy's existing productive capacity; it is money spent just to keep the economy in working order. Economists also remind us that such maintenance costs must be withdrawn from the output that could otherwise be used for direct consumption, or for new investments. Thus high maintenance costs mean that fewer economic resources can be devoted to what is, after all, the purpose of the system—meeting human needs—or to the overall growth of the economy. In this sense the cost of the fuel needed to run the existing energy system is also a maintenance cost, and as its price rises, the cost of maintaining the energy system increases, diverting economic resources from consumption or new investments.

Economists are well aware that such abstractions are hard to grasp, and are fond of inventing more homely, concrete examples to explain them. One would be useful here. Consider the economy of the Pilgrims in Massachusetts, much of it based on growing corn. To produce corn they planted seeds, depending on the soil's fertility and their own labor, to yield a harvest of perhaps fifty times more corn than they planted. The harvested corn was divided among three different uses: food; seed to replant the existing acreage for the next year's crop; seed to expand the crop acreage, in order to enlarge the annual output (to support the growing population). The first batch of corn represents that part of the economy's output which is consumed, and contributes directly to the Pilgrims' standard of living; the second batch is a maintenance cost—output used to maintain the present level of corn production; the third batch is output used to expand production—for new investment, so to speak. The total amount of corn available for these purposes, the size of the harvest, is fixed and if more is used for one purpose, less is left for the others. For example, if an inopportune storm washes out the planted corn, so that a second batch of seeds must be planted, less corn will be available for food or for new, expanded planting. In the same way, if too much corn is eaten, there will be less left to expand production, or even to maintain it.

In our own example, the economic resources needed to meet the rising cost of fuel in the present nonrenewable energy system, or to replace it with a renewable one, are like the seed corn planted for next year's crop—they represent a cost of maintaining current production. When $5 billion is invested in the energy system—whether to meet the rising cost of conventional fuel or to build one breeder or one million cogenerators—it merely maintains the economic system's productive capacity, and leaves that much less for personal consumption or for investment in new production. The cost of maintaining the energy system is a drain—albeit a necessary one—on the goods and services that are available to meet human need, which is, after all, the end purpose of the economy.

Accordingly, the economic consequences of the choice between a breeder and a solar energy system will depend on two things: their relative cost (which will determine the price for replacing the present energy system), and how soon they can be put in place (which will determine how long we will need to bear the cost of increasingly expensive fuel). There is no way at present to estimate the total cost of these systems except to say that either one would be very large. However, we do know a good deal about how soon they can be introduced. As we have seen, the major, sensible solar energy sources can be quickly introduced, some at once, and others within a few years. In contrast, no one expects breeders to be commercially available until well into the next century, perhaps twenty-five years from now, if then. By that time, the cost of conventional energy will be four to five times higher than it is now. Each year's delay in replacing the present system means spending much more to produce the same amount of conventional energy, and diverting that many more economic resources from consumption and new enterprises. Thus the three sectors—maintenance of the energy system, consumption, and new investments—compete strongly for the total output of the economic system. How different energy policies would affect the various interest groups—consumers, labor, farmers, the industries that use energy, and the industries that produce it—hinges on how each of them depends on these competing uses of the available economic resources.

If the heavy burden of the energy crisis on consumers is to be relieved, the present energy system must be replaced by one based on a source that is renewable (so that its price is stable), thrifty in its demand for economic resources (so that consumers can have access to their share), and benign in its effect on the environment (so that people can live in it without fearing for their health and safety). It seems evident that a solar energy system would serve these consumers' needs much better than one based on breeders. Because of problems inherent in its centralized design, the breeder system would use capital less efficiently than a solar system. It would generate serious environmental hazards and the risk of catastrophic accidents. It would intensify consumers' onerous dependence on the electric utilities, which have already laid claim to so large a part of people's budgets, especially among the poor.

But most important, the solar system could be introduced much sooner than the breeder system, avoiding the huge additional cost of conventional energy that will occur until it is replaced by a renewable source. The early introduction of the solar system would leave a larger part of the output of the economic system available for consumer purchases—that is, to maintain the standard of living—and for new investment to expand the economy. The transitional process would also benefit consumers. The introduction of cogenerators would reduce consumers' energy costs, and with more natural gas available, they could use that fuel for heat instead of much more expensive electricity. Finally, whereas the shift to breeders would degrade the environment, the solar transition would improve it.

Farmers are both consumers and producers. As consumers, their interests are about the same as those of consumers generally and, for the reasons already cited, will be much better served by a solar system than by a breeder system. As producers, farmers have a very special interest in solar energy. They would quickly benefit from a solar transition, which would give them immediate access to solar energy produced on the farm: alcohol and methane, and electricity from cogenerators driven by these fuels. Farmers could then regain the energy independence they once enjoyed; not by returning to draft horses and manual water pumps, but by producing for themselves the forms of energy needed to run the farm's modern equipment—tractors, trucks, grain driers, electric milking machines, refrigerators, as well as the farmhouse water pump, vacuum cleaner, and TV set. The solar fuels could be produced at a constant cost, while the price of conventional fuels escalates. So, as they shift to solar fuels, farmers could hold down their production costs and become less vulnerable to the economic difficulties they face whenever the price of farm commodities fluctuates downward. And as the price of nonrenewable fuels continues upward, and farmers begin to produce more energy than they need, they could turn the tables on the oil industry. Instead of depending on the industry's increasingly costly products, farmers could compete with them, selling not only food, but significant amounts of solar fuels as well. This would give farmers a broader, more stable market for their goods, and a new, more independent, economically secure position in the national economy.

Labor unions are frequently wooed by utilities that seek allies in their battles against citizens who oppose the construction of power plants. The utilities argue that workers need jobs and that unless energy is available, factories will close and people will be put out of work. But the real interests of working people in energy are not encompassed by this simplistic approach. It is, of course, true that energy is essential to the nation's system of production, which is in turn the source of jobs and wages. But labor has other requirements of the system of production, which may be better met by one source of energy than by another.

A renewable energy system based on breeder reactors would not serve the interests of working people very well. The heavy expenditures for nonrenewable energy during the twenty-five-year delay before breeders could be introduced would divert economic resources from the development of new industry—and the creation of new jobs. And even before breeders could be built, in the transitional period, as the electric power system expands, many industries would be forced to make unproductive investments in order to switch from natural gas (which is now widely used in industry) to electric power. This would further limit the economic resources available for new industrial investments, and whereas capital spent to build a factory will create additional jobs, capital spent on switching from one fuel to another will not (it is a maintenance cost). In contrast, in the solar transition the supply of natural gas (gradually replaced by solar methane) would expand rather than contract, and industries that depend on it could avoid such unproductive switching costs, leaving more capital for new, job-producing investments.

These considerations apply with equal force to the interests of the entrepreneurs and managers of industry generally, the productive operations that *use* energy. In recent years many industries have been hurt as energy supplies have become less certain and more costly. During the previous oil shortage caused by the 1973 embargo, some plants shut down for weeks at a time, as they did when natural gas supplies to the Midwest were disrupted in the winter of 1976–77. These events dramatized a basic fact about the relationship between the industries that use energy and the industries that produce it. Since all industries *must* have energy, the energy-producing industries are in an unchallengeable position to dictate the terms of trade. Although an appliance factory in New England might find it particularly useful to burn natural gas in its paint driers, it may be forced to use electricity or fuel oil because the gas industry has seen fit to direct its supplies elsewhere. And an industry that does get a gas hookup, and installs machinery designed to operate on it, must thereafter pay whatever price the gas company is allowed to charge, or else bear the cost of installing new equipment. Energy users have little opportunity to shop around for cheaper supplies, for even where there are multiple suppliers, as in the oil industry, their collective control of the rate of crude oil production and of refinery operations maintains a nearly uniform system of prices. In effect, in their relation to the energy-using industries, the energy-producing industries can exert most of the economic control enjoyed by a monopoly. The need to constrain this power is the reason for government regulation of the energy industry.

The energy-using industries would be better served by a solar transition than by a transition to a breeder-based system. The breeder system would require the many industries that now use liquid and gaseous fuels to redesign for electricity. This would intensify the energy industry's monopoly power since there would then be only one source of energy, under the control of large, financially powerful corporations. In contrast, the solar transition would break the hold of the energy companies over the rest of industry. In a solar system, many industries could control their own source of energy, which could often be produced locally by the industry itself or by nearby small-scale producers. A factory equipped with its own photovoltaic cells controls its source of power. A cannery that produces methane from its wastes and has a two-way connection to a methane pipeline is at least a partner in its energy supply. But once more, the most important difference between the two alternative routes to renewable energy is that the solar system would come into action sooner, so that less of the economy's resources would be drained off for maintenance of the energy system and more would be left for new industrial investment.

Thus many of the serious economic problems that now confront consumers, labor, farmers, and production industries could be resolved if the nation would embark on a transition to renewable, solar energy. Consumers would be relieved of the burden of ever-rising utility rates, and of the effects of inflation generally; they would have more money to spend on other things; their standard of living would be improved. Workers would have more job opportunities in new industries, and the high levels of unemployment that are now taken for granted could be reduced. Farmers could cut production costs and increase income by producing solar fuels, helping to reverse a twenty-five-year trend which has reduced the farmer's share of the national economy. Industries in general, which all use energy, could break out of the economic grip of the energy industry, producing energy for themselves, or purchasing it from a much wider array of sources at a stable price. Everyone would benefit from a sharp reduction in the environmental degradation that has until now accompanied the production and use of energy. The country would free itself of the fear of another Harrisburg accident or worse.

Where do the interests of the *energy-producing* industries lie in the choice between the two optional routes toward a national system of renewable energy? Among these industries there are three that together encompass all the sector's activities: electric utilities, on which all of the nuclear power industry and most of coal production depends; the gas utilities, on which the production and distribution of natural gas depends; the oil industry, which produces and sells crude oil, natural gas, and refinery products such as fuel oil and gasoline.

The electric utilities operate highly centralized power plants, and since this is precisely the design required by a breeder system, there is a nice fit between the two. But building breeders would also aggravate the utilities' two main problems—difficulties in raising capital and in meeting environmental standards. Neither of these problems could be solved by the utilities without government help. Before breeders were introduced, the government would need to shore up the faltering nuclear power industry, which, even before the accident at Harrisburg, was on the verge of collapse because it lacked sufficient orders. One possibility—already suggested by the Westinghouse Corporation—is that the government should itself buy the nuclear power plants, for later resale to utilities. Another likely maneuver, which has already been proposed by the administration, is to shorten the time required for nuclear plant construction by limiting environmental challenges. If breeders were built, these economic and environmental problems would become worse rather than better. Thus the transition to a breeder-based renewable energy system would serve the interests of the electric utilities, but only if they had a great deal of help from the government.

Even with government help, it is difficult to see how the electric utilities could survive a solar transition as viable private enterprises. To begin with, the expanded use of the solar bridging fuel, natural gas, would favor the electric utilities' only present competitors—the gas utilities (although some utilities sell both gas and electric power). New housing developments and industries would tend to install gas-driven cogenerators rather than link up to the electric utilities. (In New York, the electric utility, Consolidated Edison, is bitterly opposed to a plan to install diesel-driven cogenerators in a large office building.) Then, as solar devices are introduced, the competition would increase. And because of their particular financial structure, new competition is fatal for electric utilities. Suppose, for example, production of photovoltaic cells is expanded and their price falls enough to make them competitive with utility power. Some of the utility's customers would begin to switch to photovoltaic systems, and the demand for utility power would decline. However, as a franchised public utility, the power company is allowed a certain fixed rate of return on its capital investment, so that as the demand for power falls, the utility can compensate by *raising its rates*. (This has already happened in a number of instances, where conservation measures have reduced demand. One reason electric rates are rising so rapidly is that demand has not increased as fast as was assumed. On the average, utilities are now using only 70 percent of their capacity, but the consumers pay for the capital cost of the total capacity.) But as the utility's rates go up, the photovoltaic option will become more attractive to its customers and more of them will switch to photovoltaics. Demand will fall even more; the utility will again raise its rates; more customers will go solar. And so on. Thus, in the solar transition, the utilities' effort to maintain their rate of return in the face of growing competition will set up a feedback process that can only end with absurdly high rates—and no customers. Unless they acquired some other source of income, a national commitment to the solar transition would guarantee the demise of electric utilities as viable private investments.

However, the utilities' power lines and some of their power plants would have an important—if not financially rewarding—role to play in the solar transition. Both energy and capital can be conserved by tying a solar installation into the utilities' power grid. In a mixed solar/conventional system, the high cost of a storage system can be reduced if utility power is available as backup. Energy can be saved if a solar source can feed electricity into the power grid when it is not needed locally. However, electric utilities would hardly need to be expanded to provide such services, and unless they can grow, they are unlikely to attract sufficient private capital to remain viable. In the solar transition, some other means would need to be found to maintain these services.

The interests of the utilities that distribute natural gas are self-evident. In a transition to a breeder-based system, the (presumably) stable price of the system's renewable electricity would compete more and more successfully with natural gas, which would become exponentially more expensive. The gas utilities would be phased out gradually in such a transition. In contrast, in a solar transition the gas utilities would be the purveyors of the essential bridging fuel, natural gas, and they would flourish. Their crucial role would continue into the solar system itself, since the methane gradually added to gas pipelines from new, solar sources would be distributed through their pipelines.

Where do the interests of the oil companies lie in a possible transition to a system of renewable energy? In either a solar or a breeder transition, oil and natural gas would be needed until the renewable source was large enough to take over. But in the long run, when the solar transition is complete, only stand-by natural gas production would be needed—not much of a prospect for the huge oil companies. However, in a transition to the breeder system, their prospects would be much better. The major oil companies own a considerable part of the nation's reserves of both coal (the bridging fuel in the transition) and uranium (a breeder fuel). (According to Alfred F. Dougherty, Jr., of the Federal Trade Commission, eleven oil and gas corporations now control 51 percent of the known uranium reserves, and fourteen of the twenty major corporations now holding coal reserves are oil companies.) Thus, in a breeder transition, the major oil companies would be in an excellent position to continue to serve, as they do now, as the main suppliers of essential fuels. Moreover, since the oil companies are among the largest, wealthiest corporations in the U.S., they might invest directly in the construction of breeders, which will call for very large amounts of capital.

In a transition to a solar system, oil companies would seem to have no advantages over any other holders of investment capital, but in certain ways they would find the transition inimical to their own special interests. First, the emphasis on natural gas as the bridging fuel and the early elimination of nuclear power would tend to reduce the value of the companies' large uranium holdings. On the other hand, insofar as they hold natural gas reserves, the oil companies could play an important role in the solar transition. However, natural gas production has often been a sideline for the major oil companies, developed only as an adjunct to oil production; many of the U.S. gas producers are relatively small "independents," especially in the areas of "unconventional" gas reserves. The large oil companies therefore would have a good deal of competition in the production of natural gas, and they are more likely to invest in areas where their enormous wealth gives them a strong competitive advantage. If the oil companies were to engage in the production of solar energy devices, their huge capital resources would not be particularly advantageous, because the investments would tend to be diverse and relatively small-scaled. Thus the major oil companies are not likely to find a role in the solar transition that is suitable to their distinctive capabilities, in particular their ability to make very large investments.

In fact, the major oil companies are most likely to prefer neither of the renewable energy options. In recent years, as the price of energy has increased and oil company profits have risen, they have shown a growing interest in investing outside the field of energy. In November 1978, a survey of current trends in the oil industry by the trade magazine, *The Oil and Gas Journal,* reported: "With [oil] price increases, companies like Exxon Corp. and Phillips Petroleum Co. are generating such massive cash flows that traditional investment areas can't absorb the capital." The report continued:

> what's in store ten years from now? The latter question is perhaps more critical in the oil industry than in other businesses because it looms against a backdrop of shrinking U.S. oil and gas reserves. And there are critical decisions to be made, such as what to do with cash flows from present investments as opportunities in traditional investment areas decline.

The oil companies' cash is already beginning to flow out of oil and natural gas production. In the last few years, inflated oil company profits have been used by Mobil to acquire Montgomery Ward and Container Corp.; by Atlantic Richfield to buy Anaconda Copper and the London *Observer;* by Sun Oil to acquire a manufacturer of medical equipment; by Exxon to invest heavily in electronics; while Gulf Oil tried but failed to buy the Barnum & Bailey circus. At the same time, most of the major oil companies are increasing their already appreciable investments in chemical production. Such purchases diversify the oil company holdings, and according to a vice president of Standard Oil of California, "The thrust for

diversification comes from the depletion of oil and gas resources." The *Oil and Gas Journal* report also emphasizes the oil companies' view that investment in oil and gas production has become increasingly risky ". . . as we try to produce more difficult wells." Finally, although the industry has been drilling more domestic oil wells in the last few years because of the sharp rise in the price of oil, this will go on only if prices *continue* to rise fast enough. As one major oil company points out,

> these investments [in new U.S. oil production] are being made in anticipation of prices rising over time to what we consider to be more rational levels. If these price increases do not come about, our economics on current projects will be seriously affected, and our ability and willingness to make future investments will be greatly decreased.

The chief executive officer of one of the country's largest oil companies—John E. Sweringen of Standard Oil Company (Indiana)—has been very explicit about the reason why oil companies diversify into other areas. In an interview with the Chicago *Tribune* he said: "We're not in the energy business. We're in the business of trying to use the assets entrusted to us by our shareholders to give them the best return on the money they've invested in the company." Motivated by this philosophy, Mr. Sweringen has pushed his company into the chemical business, especially to produce raw materials for synthetic fibers, which, according to the *Tribune* interview is ". . . an investment which Wall Street analysts expect to pay off handsomely in the 1980s."

Thus, although the rising price of oil has generated unprecedented profits for the oil companies, they are increasingly reluctant to use them for "traditional investments"—that is, for the production of more oil and gas. This is the natural, inevitable outcome of the nonrenewability of these energy sources. As the deposits become progressively more costly to produce, unless the companies can be *certain* that the price of oil and gas will keep pace, they run the risk that their profits will fall. As the 1972 report of the National Petroleum Council pointed out, if the price of domestic oil had not begun to rise exponentially after that date, the oil companies' rate of return on their investment would have dropped to 2 percent by 1985.

The oil companies' uncertainty about their future profits is not surprising. They know from past experience that because oil and gas are so crucial to the economy, there is always the possibility—depending on the political outlook in Washington—that prices will be controlled. Because of this uncertainty, and the certainty that production costs will rise exponentially as oil and gas deposits are depleted, future investments in these resources are bound to become increasingly risky. The oil companies fought hard (and successfully) to deregulate natural gas, and are now agitating against the renewal of the oil price control legislation that expires in 1979 so that they can be more confident of higher future prices. For the same reason, they are heavily engaged in advertising campaigns to persuade the public that resolving the energy crisis depends on increased production, which can occur only—they say—if government regulations, especially on prices and environmental controls, are lifted.

It may seem paradoxical that while they stridently demand unrestrained control over the economics of oil and gas production as though their survival depended on it, the oil companies are quietly buying their way into other industries. But the two campaigns are in fact quite complementary: the faster energy prices rise, the more ready cash the oil companies will have to buy up other industries. This strategy would benefit from a national decision to take the breeder route, for it would give the oil companies an additional twenty-five years or more in which to collect high prices for oil and gas, and to invest the growing profits elsewhere, meanwhile profiting as well from their extensive holdings of coal and uranium.

We can now take stock of how the choice between the two optional routes to a renewable energy system is likely to affect the special interests of the different sectors of the economy. The breeder route would favor the electric utilities and the oil companies. The solar route would favor the gas utilities and all the users of energy: industry, commerce, transportation, farmers, labor, and consumers. It seems clear that the self-interest of the preponderant majority would be best served by the solar choice. Obviously, the electric utilities and the major oil companies would resist this decision and a major conflict

would arise. But the national welfare requires that the conflict be resolved, and it is useful to consider how that might be done.

To begin with, if the solar transition is to proceed smoothly, without disastrous breaks in the flow of energy, in the first half of the fifty-year transitional period the present annual rate of production of coal and domestic oil would have to be maintained, and then, along with nuclear power, gradually reduced to zero in the second half. (But nuclear power or oil imports could be phased out in the first twenty-five years.) In the first half of the transition, the annual production of natural gas would have to be nearly doubled, then allowed to decline to a low, stand-by rate in the next twenty-five years. During the transition, as oil and natural gas deposits become less accessible and more difficult to exploit, the cost of producing them, and the riskiness of the necessary investments, will rise rapidly. But despite these difficulties, the nation will have to be absolutely assured of a continuous supply of these fuels.

Under these circumstances the distributors of natural gas would flourish. As the national energy system becomes increasingly dependent on them, they would enjoy a powerful monopolistic position, which would, of course, require social control. However, this should cause no serious difficulties, since, as a public utility, the industry is already under a suitable system of regulation.

In contrast, the electric utilities' natural monopoly would end and they would rapidly lose business. Nevertheless, their facilities would be needed as a backup and distribution system for solar installations. This situation resembles the recent history of the railroads, which once had an effective monopoly on interurban transportation, and like the electric power companies, operate as a utility: the types of service offered and the rates charged are regulated by the government. But extensive automobile, truck, and air traffic broke the railroads' monopoly, and the more vulnerable ones, in the East, became unprofitable and went bankrupt. However, their freight operations and certain of their passenger operations are essential to the national economy and had to be continued. (Indeed, in any sensible energy transition the railroads should be expanded vastly and electrified.) Publicly funded corporations, Amtrak and Conrail, were created to continue at least minimal rail services. For all their inadequacies, these corporations have the merit of sustaining an essential national service which has become too un-profitable to warrant support as a private enter-prise. It is likely that in the solar transition a simi-lar fate awaits the electric utilities.

The fate of the oil companies in the solar transi-tion is a far more formidable problem. Clearly, the interests of the oil industry and of the nation as a whole are not the same. The oil industries argue that if price controls are removed and the "free market" is allowed to operate, they will have enough income to provide the "incentive" to pro-duce more oil and natural gas. But thus far they have shown a strong inclination to invest much of their profits in quite different enterprises. This runs counter to the nation's needs. What the na-tion needs, in the solar transition, is that the oil companies should serve the purposes of that tran-sition: continued production of oil and expanded production of natural gas should be *guaranteed;* the monopolistic position of the industry should not be exploited to raise prices even faster than is necessary to meet rising production costs; profits should be reinvested exclusively in more oil and gas production.

Not only are the interests of the oil companies and the nation in conflict; both parties are also uncertain of the other's behavior. The oil compa-nies fear that because of the crucial importance of their products to the national welfare, even if all controls were now lifted there is always the danger that, in the natural permutations of poli-tics, they will be reimposed. On the other hand, given the recent behavior of the oil companies, the nation has reason to distrust their willingness to reinvest in oil and gas production unless they are certain of prices that they regard as "reason-able." There is, then, a deadlock between the in-terests of the oil companies and those of the na-tion. The oil companies want a guarantee—that prices will *never* be regulated—which no one can give them; the nation needs a guarantee that the companies will continue to produce oil and gas, but they are unwilling to give that guarantee un-less prices are unregulated, if then.

This sort of situation has arisen before in con-nection with essential public services—such as electric, gas, and telephone services—that tend to be natural monopolies. Here the problem is solved by a *quid pro quo.* The companies guaran-tee to provide the needed services and in return they are granted a monopoly and the right to charge prices that give them a guaranteed but fixed rate of return on their investment. This is the familiar formula for establishing a public utility. Simply stated, then, in order to meet the national requirements for the continued produc-tion of oil and especially of natural gas during the solar transition, the companies engaged in per-forming that service would have to be given the status of public utilities, guaranteeing to devote themselves solely to the production of these fuels, and in turn guaranteed a fixed rate of return on their investment. In a basic sense, this is the inev-itable outcome of the nonrenewability of oil and natural gas. As the supplies are depleted, produc-ing these fuels becomes not only exponentially more costly but also exponentially more risky. It is an established maxim in U.S. business circles that high-risk investments (such as the develop-ment of nuclear power or of integrated circuits before there is an assured market for these prod-ucts) are inappropriate areas of private invest-ment unless supported by government financial guarantees.

Unfortunately, the major oil companies, which are accustomed to using their huge wealth and power in whatever way seems, to them, to best serve their interests, are not likely to accept the far more docile and economically settled role of a public utility. It is highly unlikely, for example, that the oil companies would support legislation that empowered them only to produce oil and nat-ural gas, at prices that guaranteed them a set rate of return. Given their strenuous objections to the much lighter level of social governance that is involved in simple price control, it is quite proba-ble that the major oil companies would rather move into other areas of investment than agree to become public energy utilities. On the other hand, the public utilities that now distribute natural gas, which are already accustomed to this status, might be quite willing to expand their operations to include the production of natural gas. (Some of these utilities already produce their own natural gas supplies, but thus far on a very small scale.)

One possible solution, then, would be to convert those companies that wished to remain in the oil and natural gas business into public utilities, ac-cepting the likelihood that the major oil compa-nies would take their cash into more attractive areas of investment. However, one can foresee certain moral objections to allowing the oil com-panies to take over other industries, for this would reward the industry that has profited most from the energy crisis and punish the far more numerous industries that have been hurt by it. Ironically, it is the energy crisis itself that has given the major oil companies the opportunity to invade new sectors of the economy. By their own admission, the crisis has enabled them to accumulate more capital than they are now willing to reinvest in oil and gas production. At the same time, the energy crisis has helped to weaken the rest of the economy, so that other companies can now be bought up at bargain prices. This is reminiscent of what happened in the Great Depression, when the larger, wealthier, more viable companies bought out those that weakened and failed. This time, however, the process could be halted, or at least mitigated, by undertaking the solar transition, for that would slow down, and eventually end, the escalation of energy prices, which is the source of the oil companies' financial power.

Thus the decision to embark at once on the solar transition would mean an unavoidable clash between the national interest and the special interests of the major oil companies and the electric utilities. In the solar transition, the major oil companies, among the richest and most powerful corporations in the U.S., or the world, would lose their dominant position in the economy. For them, the transition would end the attractive prospect of at least twenty-five more years of escalating energy prices, which—given their rights as private entrepreneurs—would enable them to accumulate huge profits and buy up ever larger sectors of the economy. When a solar energy system is in place, and renewable sources have largely replaced oil and natural gas, the oil companies' economic role would become limited to production of stand-by natural gas and raw materials for the chemical industry. (But here, too, if biomass production could be enlarged sufficiently, these biological sources might even replace oil and natural gas as basic chemical feedstocks.) On the other hand, if the interests of the oil companies prevailed and the solar transition is delayed or blocked entirely, they would continue to flourish while the rest of the economy would suffer. Conversely, the rest of industry, and indeed the economy as a whole, would clearly benefit from the solar transition. Damage to the private interests of the major oil companies seems to be a necessary cost of these larger, social benefits. As

economists would say: there is no free lunch.

There is a similar clash between social interest and the private interest of the other industry that would be hurt by the solar transition—the electric utilities. This conflict has already become severe, as the utilities attempt to compensate for their worsening economic efficiency by placing the resultant burden on consumers. In 1977 electric utilities had 50 percent more surplus capacity than they needed as a safety margin to ensure a continuous supply of power, partly because they overestimated demand, partly because their plants' large capacity outruns even the accurately estimated demand, and partly because they built nuclear power plants, which are less efficient than coal-fired plants. Since rates are based on the capital cost of equipment whether it is fully used or not, this inefficiency has contributed to high rates, thus forcing consumers to pay for the utilities' mistakes. A recent rate controversy between Consolidated Edison and its customers in New York is a particularly illuminating example of this conflict. To resolve the dispute, two Public Service Commission administrative law judges recommended a large rate increase, while conceding that it would "pose a hardship to consumers." But they justified their action as follows:

The root problem may be that our society's conception of social justice is unworkable in tandem with its economic structure. If a day of reckoning is inevitable, perhaps its coming should be hastened rather than retarded, so that we can proceed with our next experiment in civilization.

The conflict between social justice and the private governance of the economic system is the root problem not only of utility costs, but also of the energy crisis itself. Perhaps this can best be seen from the perspective of history—in particular, the origin of the National Energy Plan in the historical event that immediately preceded its creation: the election of 1976. As soon as Mr. Carter took office he urgently ordered his staff to produce the Plan. At first blush this would suggest that action on the energy crisis was a major mandate emerging out of the presidential campaign. But in fact, in the 1976 campaign neither candidate made an effort to create a mandate on energy, or for that matter on any other issue. The campaign was widely regarded as a hodgepodge of trivia. When *The New York Times* announced its support for Mr. Carter, it complained that both contestants were "unable in three national televised debates adequately to articulate their respective philosophies of government or to clarify the political, economic and moral issues that divide them." The *Wall Street Journal,* which supported Gerald Ford, introduced a series of editorials on the election by declaring: "Well, if the candidates aren't going to talk about the issues, somebody ought to."

But just because the candidates did not discuss the issues does not mean that there were none. History warns against that simple conclusion. The United States has suffered through a number of such banal presidential campaigns, not because the country was free of trouble, but because it was deeply divided over a great issue—which the candidates tried to avoid. Historians point out that the successive elections between 1840 and 1856 of those hard-to-remember Presidents—Harrison, Polk, Taylor, Pierce, and Buchanan—were the results of monumentally trivial campaigns. The campaigns were trivial because the candidates were desperately trying to avoid the one issue that really troubled the country. Only with Lincoln's candidacy in 1860 was the long-evaded issue put before the electorate: slavery.

Like the campaigns that marked what the historian James Morgan has called the "ignominious era which opened with the accession of Tyler and ended with the inauguration of Lincoln," the 1976 campaign was also an exercise in the politics of evasion. But the hidden issue can be found in the rubble of Carter's energy plan. The Plan failed because, like the campaign, it ignored the same "root problem" that troubled the judges in the Consolidated Edison rate case: the clash between social justice and the structure of the economy; between the national interest and the private interests of the energy industry. This conflict arises because the energy system, like the production system as a whole, is essential to national welfare, but is governed by private rather than social interests. In recent years it has become an article of faith that the instrument of social interest, the government, is to be called upon to produce needed goods or services—even those as unsuitable to the private sector as postal service—only as a last resort, and even then with misgivings. Under this constraint, which Mr. Carter made a precondition of his energy policy, all the Plan could do was to manipulate private economic interests by offering financial inducements and threatening financial penalties. This strategy yielded only small returns, such as minor energy savings through improved insulation, and even smaller gains in solar energy for hot water. The programs that could have had a much larger impact on the energy situation, but would have required social intervention—such as mass transit, large-scale production of solar fuels, or a photovoltaic purchase plan—are conspicuously absent from the Plan. And even after the Plan's failure to deal with the basic energy problem—the relation between production of energy and its price—became too conspicuous to ignore, Mr. Carter could think only of private interest, tempered by the puny threat of antitrust laws, as the answer. At his January 29, 1979, press conference, he was asked:

Mr. President, the fourth quarter profits are out for the big oil companies . . . they reached 48 percent, 72 percent, 44 percent, 134 percent increases over profits in the same period last year. . . . I was wondering if you would give us your reaction to these profits—profits that rise when American workers are being asked to hold wage increases to 7 percent.

And Mr. Carter replied:

. . . whether the free enterprise system with competition, and a rigid application of antitrust laws, can induce both increased production and therefore more competition, and lower prices, I can't anticipate.

Here Mr. Carter accurately reflects how decisions about the design of the production system—whether oil companies produce foreign or domestic oil; whether auto manufacturers build large cars or small ones, whether home builders install gas or electric heat—are made. Such decisions are made solely by the producers of the goods, narrowly guided by the principle that governs all private economic decisions—profitability. However, the nation's experience with energy problems—and with environmental problems before them—has shown that when production decisions are made in this simple, autonomous way, they are likely to ignore grave social consequences, which are regarded as "externalities," factors that are irrelevant to private transactions. But while this principle serves the private interests, it damages the social ones. Thus, when U.S. oil companies shifted their hunt for oil from domestic to foreign areas in the 1950s, the companies benefited (for a number of years the rate of profit on their foreign operations was twice the profit on their domestic ones), but the nation bears the burden of threatened embargoes and a negative balance of trade. When, after World War II, the auto companies decided to build larger cars, they profited (the rate of profit was much larger on big cars than on little ones), but gas mileage fell and the country's oil reserves were depleted more rapidly. And in recent years, as new homes have increasingly been equipped with electric heat—the most wasteful form of energy for that purpose—the builders' costs were held down (electric heaters are cheaper than a gas heat system), but more fuel had to be burned, and more air was polluted, than before. In all these enterprises private interests gained and the national, social interest suffered.

The outcome of the solar transition also depends a great deal on whether it would be governed by private or social interests. As we have seen, because conventional energy sources are rising exponentially in price, it is advantageous to switch to solar energy (which will remain constant in price) as soon as the conventional and solar cost curves cross. There are two alternative ways to hasten the crossover. One strategy would rely on private interest, operating through the "free marketplace," to govern the introduction of solar technologies. The price of conventional energy would be unregulated and allowed to rise as fast as the energy companies' monopoly position can drive it. That is why some solar energy enthusiasts favored the National Energy Plan—which was designed to allow the highest-priced market for fuel, the international oil market, to set the price of domestic energy. They reasoned that this strategy would increase the general cost of conventional energy so that solar technologies would more quickly become competitive and enter the market sooner—but at a high price. The oil companies would benefit from the higher oil and natural gas prices. Wealthy people would benefit too, for they could afford the solar investment and so avoid buying high-priced fuel. But poor people, unable to buy expensive solar devices, would be forced to pay higher prices for conventional fuel. This approach to the solar transition is Robin Hood in reverse; it would help the rich

and hurt the poor, justifying the suspicion that public movements for energy conservation and solar energy are elitist.

The alternative strategy would rely instead on social interest, by deliberately using public funds to reduce the cost of those solar technologies that are most important to the solar transition, and to its broad, social benefits. Public funds could be used for the initial purchase needed to establish new, competitive solar industries (for example, the proposed federal photovoltaic purchase plan); or to finance solar public works (for example, to construct municipal plants to convert garbage and sewage to methane); or to subsidize solar innovations in housing, agriculture, and transportation. By speeding the development of solar alternatives to increasingly expensive nonrenewable fuels, this strategy would hold down overall energy costs rather than increase them.

In such a strategy of social governance, public agencies, responsible to the citizens, would decide which solar technologies ought to be introduced, and when. These judgments would rely not only on the technology's immediate cost-effectiveness, or on its profitability to the producer, but more crucially, on its *social* value in fostering an effective overall solar transition. Such a strategy would permit rational planning of the development, testing, and introduction of solar technologies in keeping with the national interest in a smooth, rapid solar transition, rather than conforming only to the narrow criterion of private profitability. But it would challenge the great American taboo against even hinting that social welfare might be a better reason for a new productive investment than private profit.

Here we can see another parallel between the energy crisis and the slavery question: Both concern the issue of social governance of the system of production. Apart from its moral and political connotations, slavery is the use of a particular form of energy—slave labor—in production. And indeed, a good deal of the opposition to slavery was based on the inefficiencies that it imposed on production, not only in the South, but nationally. Allan Nevins, the historian, cites a prominent Kentuckian's view that in Virginia, "the clog that has stayed the march of her people, the incubus that has weighed down her enterprise, strangled her commerce, kept sealed her exhaustless fountain of mineral wealth, and paralyzed her arts, manufactures, and improvements is Negro slavery." And in the North, he tells us, in the period before the Civil War, while the politicians asked, "Could the Union endure?" the businessmen asked, "Could a truly national utilization of the country's resources be achieved?"

As long as slavery persisted and the South remained tied to an inefficient, purely agricultural economy, it was difficult to modernize national production technology. While slavery persisted the nation could not take full advantage of the industrial revolution, which before the Civil War made much faster progress in Europe than in the United States. Only with the end of slavery could the country embark upon the huge technological advance that turned it into the most productive nation in the world. But this sweeping transformation of the national system of production was not the result of private interests, trading in the "free marketplace." Rather, it was the result of a historic political decision, in which the people of the United States chose to exert social governance over the system of production by ending its access to slave labor.

Like the abolition of slavery, the solar transition would be a historic turning point in the development of the U.S. economy. This is evident from its potential impact not only on the energy situation but on the production system as a whole, and on the efficiency and growth of the economy. It is a shocking but poorly appreciated fact that the vitality of American industry, and with it the economy, has declined sharply, especially in the last decade. Once the source of numerous technological innovations, the development of new industrial products has diminished in the United States. Much industrial research is now designed to find more profitable ways to produce old products rather than to develop new ones. The replacement of production machinery has slowed down in a number of major industries, such as steel and textiles, placing them at a disadvantage in foreign trade. Just as the United States lagged behind England and Germany in industrial technology before the Civil War, now in many areas we lag behind Japan and West Germany. In a recent review of the state of the U.S. economy, Dr. Walter Heller has called attention to the serious consequences of this trend:

> But the most disturbing development is the slowdown in innovation and technological advance. We are devoting a smaller share of our national income to research and development than we did even five or ten years ago, while our competitors are devoting a larger share of theirs. Unless we can reverse that trend, this country's economic leadership of the world will be threatened.

We hardly need a scholarly analysis to reveal that the American economy is in deep trouble. In the last year the dollar has suffered a disastrous decline; inflation has rapidly eroded the standard of living; the country seems headed into a depression. There is a growing awareness that these are not temporary aberrations in a basically sound economy, but that, as a review in *The New York Times* financial section has pointed out:

> a fundamental change may be taking place in the American economy, ushering in a time of slower growth, lower investment and the need of more people to work.

It is generally acknowledged that what lies behind this fundamental change is a sharp reduction in the rate at which the efficiency of the economy has been improving. The economy's strength depends on the rate of improvement in "total productivity," or the amount of output the economy produces from a unit amount of economic resources (raw materials, energy, labor, and capital). But this rate has declined sharply; it is now about half of what it was ten years ago.

A chief reason is the shift in the way in which capital is invested in new production technologies. During the classical period of industrial development in the United States following the Civil War, productivity grew largely through the application of science and technology to the invention of new products: the automobile, the telephone, the electric light, and all the creations of the generation of inventors typified by Ford, Edison, and Bell. In recent years, however, productivity has increased not so much through the invention of new products as through the improvement of the processes by which the old ones are produced. Thus, while the basic technological design of the automobile has been unchanged for many years, there have been dramatic advances *inside* the auto factories, with the introduction of rapid, highly automated, computer-controlled operations. But this process has its limits. As production machinery becomes more automated and complex, it uses more control devices (switches, valves, meters, and so forth), which are disproportionately expensive relative to the rest of the machine. So there is a limit to the economic returns that can be gained by further automation. And there is, after all, a limit to the number of dials that one worker can watch, or the number of buttons that one worker can push, so that at some point it is no longer possible to make much economic gain by reducing the work force. Thus there seem to be limits to the gains in productivity that can be made by such changes in production processes, and in some areas of the economy we may be approaching these limits.

The partisans of private enterprise will claim that since the enormous increases in total productivity over the last century are the result of decisions governed by private interests, we can count on these same interests to reverse the current slowdown. It is certainly true that private entrepreneurs can claim credit for the huge improvements in the efficiency with which the U.S. production system converts human and natural resources into economic output. It is a fact, after all, that the automobile was developed, and the assembly line on which it is manufactured was introduced, not because the American people thought that the country would benefit, but because Henry Ford and his industrial descendants thought that *they* would profit. However, such private decisions can govern only limited segments of the overall system of production. Inside the privately governed factory, a gas-guzzling automobile can be produced with admirable efficiency. But once it is on the road, the car becomes a drag on the economy because it forces us to buy so much gasoline at an ever-increasing price. Privately owned modern electric power plants are marvels of efficiency, producing about one third more power per unit of fuel energy than they did twenty years ago. But they still waste more energy than they use, and because they are large and centralized, their "waste" heat is inaccessible to consumers, who are doomed to pay ever higher prices for their energy. Corn Belt farms now produce much more grain per unit of resources and labor invested than they used to, but because they must purchase nonrenewable energy instead of producing their own solar sources, the farmers are at the mercy of the rapidly rising cost of fuel and fertilizer, and food prices keep rising.

But our analysis of the energy crisis shows that there *are* ways to improve the efficiency of production. While we are beginning to run out of ways of improving the productivity of manufacturing and using gasoline-driven automobiles, there are enormous opportunities for improving the productivity of transportation: electric cars using batteries charged by photovoltaic cells; a national electrified railroad system, its power plants' "waste" heat used to warm homes. Although centralized power systems have reached their productive limits, there are, after all, ways of vastly improving the efficiency with which electricity is produced: a decentralized system using natural-gas- or methane-driven cogenerators, windmills, and photovoltaic cells. And although farmers may be reaching the limit of the number of bushels of corn that can be produced with one gallon of tractor fuel, they can now begin to replace it with their own solar alcohol and methane, with no loss in food production, a net gain in productivity.

The high productivity of the modern American car factory, power plant, and grain farm is certainly a tribute to the efficacy of private enterprise. But this process seems to have run its course, for now the inefficiencies that need to be overcome are not *within* each of the separate, privately governed enterprises, but in their *links* to the rest of the productive system. However, these links are "external" to private enterprise and the famous invisible hand of the free market cannot readily reach them. There is, therefore, little that private interest alone can now do to improve the overall productivity of the economic system. Now social governance is needed.

This is the chief lesson to be learned from our analysis of the energy crisis. The energy crisis—and the economic crisis that is following in its wake—is a sign that we have failed to integrate efficiently the production of energy with its use: that the links between the auto factory and the gasoline pump, between the power plant and the home, between the farm and the sun, are loose and enormously wasteful. And the solution—the solar transition—is designed to correct precisely these faults by creating links that integrate the different sources of solar energy intimately into the production processes that can best use them. That is why the solar transition means a vast improvement in the efficiency with which resources are used, in productivity and in economic output. On the farm, the solar transition means an end to the wasteful, unnecessary use of energy-intensive inputs, producing appreciable amounts of energy without reducing food production—a larger economic output from the same agricultural resources. In the city, the solar transition means replacing inherently inefficient, centralized power plants with local cogenerators, so that homes and shops can be heated, cooled, and lighted more efficiently and more cheaply—a higher standard of living for consumers. In the factories, the solar transition means a more efficient match between energy and the energy-using tasks of production—greater industrial productivity. The solar transition means that economic resources now wastefully tied up in maintaining an energy system that threatens to cannibalize the rest of the economy can be released and put to useful work: building solar collectors; alcohol plants; methane generators; photovoltaic cells; windmills; cogenerators; electrified railroads, and urban electric trolley systems.

In sum, the solar transition offers the nation a momentous opportunity, which like the decision to abolish slavery, can rebuild the faltering economy. But it is beyond the reach of purely private governance. Society as a whole must be involved, for the solar transition is a great historic passage which only the people of the United States can decide to undertake. What stands in the way of that decision is neither technology nor economics, but politics—the politics of evasion, which, by denying that the problem exists, deprives the American people of the opportunity to solve it. In January 1977, with the nation already jolted by rising energy costs, well into an escalating course of inflation, and on the brink of a disastrous economic decline, Mr. Carter's inaugural address might well have been described as follows:

The President's address, though not without a decorous note of humility, breathed firm self-confidence, and showed that he neither recognized any grave problem before the nation nor proposed any policy that would create new issues. . . . He laid stress on the importance of integrity and economy in the public service.

But in fact this is Allan Nevins's account of the inaugural address of President Franklin Pierce in 1853. (What Mr. Carter did say in his own address was: "I have no new dreams to set forth today, but rather urge faith in the old dream. . . . we can neither answer all questions nor solve all problems. We cannot afford to do everything . . .") Both Presidents were practicing the politics of evasion. But the fault lies with neither Pierce nor Carter; both accurately reflected the temper of the parties that chose them. Indeed, nowhere in the sordid history of the National Energy Plan is there evidence that its failings were due to anything as simple as personal greed or corruption on the part of administration officials. The fault lies deeper: in the present structure of the political system that has given Mr. Carter and the administration their power.

If, as Nevins tells us of the elections of 1852, "personalities and party loyalty, not questions of public policy, would decide the coming contest," the same can surely be said of the election of 1976. The two present parties seem to be devoted not so much to the development of national policy as to electing their candidates, using whatever seemingly popular expedient is thought to work—cutting taxes, stopping busing, opposing abortions, or decrying the capabilities of the very government they propose to administer. The most incisive measure of its effect—voter turnout—marks this strategy as a failure. In the 1976 election, barely half the eligible voters went to the polls, a drop of 8 percentage points from 1960. It is customary to blame such lack of interest on "voter apathy," as though this were some kind of disease that dulled the voters' political senses. But in fact voters are not apathetic; rather, they are too deeply concerned with the nation's serious problems to be interested in the candidates' trivial answers. As one citizen who was interviewed by *The New York Times* during the 1976 presidential campaign put it: "The President of the U.S. isn't going to solve our problems. The problems are too big." But of course, this same idea can be put the other way around—the politicians are too small for the problems.

This may be the answer to the persistent questions that arise as one reflects on the contrast between the government's energy policy and common sense. If the crisis is due to the non-renewability of our present fuels, why has the government done so little to encourage the production of renewable fuels? If a major solar technology, such as the photovoltaic cell, is now technologically feasible and, with a relatively small expenditure of public funds, could be massively commercialized, why has Mr. Carter specifically refused to expend these funds, despite congressional authorization? If the most effective single step to conserve fuel would be the vast expansion and electrification of the railroads and urban mass transit systems, why has the government refused to consider these options, meanwhile proposing to cut Amtrak trackage in half?

The answer to each of these questions is the same: In each case the specific problem cannot be solved without violating the taboo that has thus far protected the private interests of the energy industries from the encroachment of the social interest. If the nation undertook to develop renewable solar fuels, so that fuel prices became stabilized, the oil industry would lose much of the huge profits they are certain to gain if prices continue to escalate. If photovoltaic cells became commercial, the private electric utilities would not long survive the competition. If the railroads expanded, and carried passengers, they could not operate as private, profitable enterprises and would need to be nationalized. (Most of the railroads in the rest of the world carry many passengers and operate, at a loss, as nationalized systems.) Each of these energy problems depends on the solution to a single, much larger one: social governance.

This is the problem that seems to be "too big" not only for the President, but for the Congress as well. There, apart from a few voices calling for the creation of a federal energy corporation, nothing was heard about this overriding issue during the debate on the energy plan. No "new dreams" troubled that debate, and in the absence of a clarifying vision, no sense could be made of the energy crisis.

Now, having failed to produce an energy policy capable of combating inflation rather than abetting it, the administration has prescribed a regimen of austerity for the country. The energy crisis, we are told, symbolizes a new limit to the nation's capabilities, which we must acknowledge by lowering expectations. This argument has been widely accepted, and we can already see the emerging tragedy of an era dominated, as the cover of a news weekly recently declared, by the "Politics of Austerity": Everyone accepts that the country is going into a long economic decline; that the economic pie is shrinking; that no one group can get more without another getting less. Conservative politicians want to cut social services, in order to maintain and even expand the military budget; liberal politicians want to cut the military budget, so that social services can be maintained. No one, it seems, is ready to ask why the richest nation in human history must act as though it is poor; why its citizens must fight over who will suffer least from this counterfeit poverty.

And now the failure to solve the energy crisis and the economic consequence of that failure are raising the specter of war. In March 1978 one of the major voices of the U.S. business community, *Business Week,* published a "Special Issue," its cover decorated by a photograph of the Statue of Liberty—with a painted tear running down its massive cheek. What is special about the issue is a long article called "The Decline of U.S. Power. The new debate over guns and butter." According to the article, "The U.S. . . . the colossus that emerged after World War II—is now clearly facing a crisis of the decay of power." The chief evidence, according to *Business Week,* is our declining influence in the Mideast, and the main reason why that is such a serious fault is that the Mideast is the key to U.S. energy supply:

> In the five years since the Organization of Petroleum Exporting Countries grabbed control of the world oil market and began to exact the wages of monopoly, American policy makers have been living in a fool's paradise, substituting rhetoric for action. . . . Faced with another oil-based bout of world-wide recession, even the most complacent of politicians must finally be persuaded that something decisive will have to be done to remove OPEC's constant threat to the world's economic system. . . . For the ultimate threat—the complete cutoff of Middle East oil—there is only one possible response.

According to the article, the "one possible response" is that recently proposed by Secretary of Defense Harold Brown: "We'll take action that's appropriate, including use of military force."

Here then are the dangerous consequences of the nation's failure, thus far, to understand, let alone solve, the energy crisis. Once we do understand the energy crisis, it becomes clear that the nation is not poor, but mismanaged; that energy is not wasted carelessly, but by design; that the energy we need is not running out, but is replenished with every dawn; that by relying on our solar resources we can forswear the suicidal prospect of a war that would begin with oil but end with a nuclear holocaust.

The solution to the energy crisis—the solar transition—is an opportunity to turn this knowledge into action, to embark on a new historic passage. But to find our way we will need to be guided by social rather than private interests. There are many known ways—and many yet to be invented—of introducing social governance into production: national planning; local or regional planning; public utilities; cooperatives; and, if need be, public ownership on a local or national level. These measures will, of course, clash with the notion that every productive decision must be privately governed, for private profit, in order to ensure economic efficiency. But we now know from the energy crisis that the inefficiencies are located outside the realm of private governance, and are accessible only to social decisions.

Here it will be argued that government enterprises are notoriously inefficient, and the Postal Service will be cited as a laughable example. Yet every vocal enemy of "government bureaucracy" who flies the U.S. airlines willingly risks his life on the efficiency, skill, and devotion of the civil servants who comprise another government bureaucracy—the Federal Aviation Administration. These examples warn us to examine the *reason* for government intervention before condemning it wholesale as a poor idea. Auto manufacturers—who now find government environmental and energy regulations so onerous—can blame these regulations on their own, private entrepreneurial decision to build large cars and to equip them with powerful high-compression engines that waste gasoline and produce smog. If, after World War II, Detroit had continued to build smaller (but less profitable) cars with low-compression engines, government regulations to reduce emissions and improve gasoline mileage—and the bureaucratic machinery created to design and enforce them—would have been unnecessary. But this could be done only if the social interest in a decent environment and the thrifty use of fuel, rather than the purely private interest in profit, had governed the relevant production decision.

It will also be argued that "social governance" would necessarily impose political constraints that would erode civil liberties and weaken democratic government. This is a serious problem, but the country does, after all, seem to have the wisdom and strength to protect our liberties from erosion or assault. In only the last two decades we have thrown back Senator McCarthy's attack on civil liberties and Mr. Nixon's powerful attempt to subvert the democratic governance of the nation.

It will be difficult—some say impossible—to learn how to merge economic justice with economic progress, and personal freedom with social governance. If we allow the fear of failing in this aim to forestall the effort to achieve it, then failure is certain. But if we firmly embrace economic democracy as a national goal, as a new standard for political policy, as a vision of the nation's future, it can guide us through the historic passage that is mandated by the energy crisis, and restore to the nation the vitality that is inherent in the richness of its resources and the wisdom of its people.

Notes

PROLOGUE

page vii: QUOTATIONS FROM CARTER SPEECH: See *The New York Times,* April 19, 1977.

page vii: WHITE HOUSE QUOTATIONS: See *The New York Times,* April 19, 1977 ("cornerstone"), and the Washington *Post,* September 9, 1978, p. 6 ("centerpiece").

page vii: SCHLESINGER QUOTATION: Speech by James R. Schlesinger to the Meeting of the Governing Board of the International Energy Act at the Ministerial Level, October 5, 1977, manuscript obtained from the press office of the U.S. Department of Energy.

page vii: *Wall Street Journal* QUOTATION: See the *Wall Street Journal,* October 16, 1978.

page vii: *The New York Times* QUOTATION: See *The New York Times,* November 19, 1978.

page vii: GEORGE F. WILL QUOTATION: See *Newsweek,* November 27, 1978, p. 120.

page vii: COVER OF *Newsweek* MAGAZINE: See *Newsweek,* January 29, 1979.

page viii: "SENIOR TREASURY OFFICIAL" QUOTATION: See *Newsweek,* February 19, 1979.

page viii: DAVID BRODER QUOTATION: See the Washington *Post,* February 18, 1979.

page viii: MARVIN STONE QUOTATION: See *U.S. News & World Report,* March 5, 1979.

page viii: HAMILTON AND CRAWFORD QUOTATIONS: See the record of the Subcommittee on Europe and the Middle East of the U.S. House of Representatives Committee on Foreign Relations, hearings on "The Proposed Arms Transfer to the Yemen Arab Republic," March 12, 1979, in publication, 1979.

page viii: CARTER ON NUCLEAR POWER: See Carter's speech on April 5, 1979, reported in *The New York Times*, April 6, 1979.

1 THE NATIONAL ENERGY PLAN: The Politics of Confusion

page 3: QUOTATIONS FROM CARTER SPEECH: See *The New York Times,* April 19, 1977. This speech (a television address on April 18, 1977) and Carter's speech to Congress on April 20, together with the *Fact Sheet,* are the basic sources for the facts about the National Energy Plan that are cited in this chapter.

page 3: Fact Sheet: See the White House, Office of the White House Press Secretary, *Detailed Fact Sheet: The President's Energy Program,* April 20, 1977. Reprinted in *The New York Times,* April 21, 1977.

page 3: CARTER'S ORDER TO STAFF: See his first interview as President, *The New York Times,* January 25, 1977.

page 3: CARTER'S SPEECH TO CONGRESS ON THE NATIONAL ENERGY PLAN ON APRIL 20, 1977: See *The New York Times,* April 21, 1977.

page 4: "EQUAL SACRIFICES": See Carter's speech on April 18, 1977.

page 4: QUOTATION ON TAX REBATE: See *Fact Sheet.*

page 4: DEFINITION OF NEW OIL: See *Fact Sheet.*

page 4: "WE MUST PROTECT THE ENVIRONMENT": See *Fact Sheet.*

page 4: QUOTATION ON ENRICHMENT GUARANTEE: See *Fact Sheet.*

page 5: AMOUNT OF OIL IMPORTED IN 1985: See *Fact Sheet.*

page 5: The National Energy Plan: Executive Office of the President, Energy Policy and Planning, *The National Energy Plan* (Washington, D.C.: U.S. Government Printing Office, April 29, 1977).

page 6: "THE CORNERSTONE OF OUR POLICY": See Carter's speech on April 18, 1977.

page 6: National Energy Plan TABLES: See *The National Energy Plan,* pp. 95–96. For a detailed analysis of the ways in which the Plan proposed to revise the national energy budget, based on the data presented in these tables and their conflict with administration claims, see Barry Commoner, *The National Energy Plan: A Critique* (Washington, D.C.: The National League of Cities, June 1977), and Barry Commoner, "The Hidden Jokers in Carter's Energy Deck," Washington *Post,* May 29, 1977.

page 6: PERCENTAGE CONTRIBUTION OF VARIOUS ENERGY SOURCES IN PLAN: See Commoner, *The National Energy Plan: A Critique,* cited above.

page 6: QUOTATION FROM FIFTH PRINCIPLE: See Carter's speech on April 18, 1977.

page 7: CONSERVATION IN TRANSPORTATION SECTOR: See Commoner, *The National Energy Plan: A Critique,* cited above.

page 7: PERCENTAGE OF ELECTRICITY USED FOR SPACE HEAT AND HOT WATER: U.S. Department of Energy/Energy Information Administration (DOE/EIA), Office of Energy Data, *End Use Energy Consumption Data Base: Series 1 Tables* (Springfield, Va.: National Technical Information Service, June 1978), pp. 21–29. DOE/EIA-0014, PB-281 817.

page 7: COMMENT ON NUMERICAL ANALYSIS: This is based on my own recollection of the event, in which I participated.

page 8: FREEMAN QUOTATION: See *The New York Times,* July 24, 1977.

page 8: QUOTATION FROM THE *Plan*: See *The National Energy Plan,* pp. 95–96.

page 8: "AN ECONOMIC, SOCIAL AND POLITICAL CRISIS": See Carter's speech on April 18, 1977.

2 "WONDER COOKIE": The Politics of Deceit

page 9: THE COSTS OF OIL WELLS AND NUCLEAR POWER PLANTS: See, for example, the study by the American Gas Association "A Comparison of Capital Investment Requirements for Alternative Domestic Energy Supplies" (Arlington, Va.: The American Gas Association [AGA], May 18, 1979). Report No. 1978-9.

page 9: QUOTATION FROM *The National Energy Plan:* See pp. 9–10 in that document, cited in Chapter 1, note for p. 5.

page 10: "WONDER COOKIE": This is the computer term for the output report of the PIES Integrating Model. For a description of the model, see Federal Energy Administration, Office of Energy Information and Analysis, "Project Independence Evaluation System (PIES) Documentation: Volume XIV, A Users Guide" (Springfield, Va.: NTIS, June 1977), p. 59. PB-268 850; FEA/N-77/115.

page 10: PUBLIC OPINION POLLS: See National Opinion Research Center, *The Impact of the 1973–74 Oil Embargo on the American Household* (Chicago, Ill.: National Opinion Research Center, 1974), p. 175.

page 10: NIXON QUOTATION: See R. Nixon, "The Energy Emergency: The President's Address to the Nation Outlining Steps to Deal with the Emergency," November 7, 1973, *Weekly Compilation of Presidential Documents IX* (July–December 1973), p. 344.

page 10: Project Independence Report: See Federal Energy Administration, *Project Independence Report* (Washington, D.C.: U.S. Government Printing Office, November 1974), pp. 18–19.

page 10: THE SIZE OF THE PIES MODEL STAFF: See Thomas H. Tietenberg, *Energy Planning and Policy* (Lexington, Mass.: Lexington Books, D. C. Heath and Company, 1976). This is a detailed insider's account of how the PIES model was produced.

page 10: PIES BIRTH QUOTATION: See ibid., pp. 63–64.

page 12: OEIA RESPONSIBILITIES: The Energy Conservation and Production Act: Public Law 94-385, August 14, 1976, amending Public Law 93-275, the Federal Energy Administration Act of 1974 (Part C, secs. 141 and 52).

page 12: "BECAUSE CONGRESS LACKED CONFIDENCE . . .": See Professional Audit Review Team, *Activities of the Office of Energy Information and Analysis (FEA)* (Washington, D.C.: U.S. Government Printing Office, December 5, 1977), p. 1. This is later referred to in the text as the "PART report."

page 12: SAFEGUARD PROVISION QUOTATION: See The Energy Conservation and Production Act, P.L. 94-385, secs. 142, 51(a) and 51(a)1 (as quoted in the PART report above).

page 12: OEIA'S FIRST ANNUAL REPORT TO CONGRESS: See Federal Energy Administration, *1976 National Energy Outlook* (Washington, D.C.: U.S. Government Printing Office, February 1976), FEA-N-75/713.

page 12: DRAFT OEIA 1977 ANNUAL REPORT: See Federal Energy Administration, *1977 National Energy Outlook, DRAFT* (Draft NEO/77 report) (Washington, D.C.: Federal Energy Administration, January 15, 1977), unpublished manuscript (available from Washington University Library [St. Louis], Federal Documents Depository).

page 12: "SINCE THE CARTER ADMINISTRATION . . .": See PART report, p. 25.

page 13: "THE EXECUTIVE OFFICE OF THE PRESIDENT'S ENERGY POLICY AND PLANNING STAFF . . .": See PART report, p. 37.

page 13: CONFERENCE ON FEBRUARY 15, 1977: This discussion is referred to in a memorandum for Alvin Alm and George Hall, from John D.Christie, routed through Christina Rathkopf on the subject of "Base Case Specifications for the President's Program." The memorandum is dated February 17, 1977, and originated in the office of the Assistant Administrator of the Federal Energy Administration (Xerox copy), p. 1. The meeting is also mentioned in the memo of February 23 (see note that follows).

page 13: QUOTATIONS FROM MEMORANDUM OF FEBRUARY 23, 1977: A memorandum for John D. Christie from George R. Hall on the subject "Base Case Specifications for the President's Program" (Xerox). The memorandum originated in the Executive Office of the President, Energy Policy and Planning. Hereafter, this is referred to as the February 23 memorandum. The quotations on p. 14 are also from this memorandum.

page 15: "DOCUMENTATION FOR THE RECORD": This is a memorandum for the files from Elizabeth Chase MacRae and John Solow of the OEIA staff on the subject of "Differences Between the Draft NEO/77 Reference Case and the President's Program Base Case for 1985" (Xerox). The memorandum was originally dated June 27, 1977, and was revised on July 25, 1977. This memorandum is referred to in the PART report.

page 15: "THE INCREASED GAP . . .": See PART report, p. 37.

page 16: CARTER QUOTATION: See *The New York Times,* April 21, 1977.

page 16: COMPARISONS OF FIGURES IN *The National Energy Plan* AND UNALTERED VERSION OF PIES: Some readers may be interested in a more detailed discussion of the origin of the various numbers cited here and elsewhere in this chapter. In chronological order, the following events occurred: First, in January 1977, OEIA published its regular annual report, "National Energy Outlook, 1977," but only in draft form. That report contains tables giving the output of the PIES model, in its then current form, regarding the U.S. energy supply and demand projected for 1985, if current policy remained in effect. This is the "Base Case" projection. As noted in the text, at this point, at the behest of the White House energy staff, a series of changes were made that significantly altered the model's predictions for the 1985 base case. These changes are tabulated in the MacRae memorandum. These *altered* predictions appear in *The National Energy Plan* tables (pp. 95 and 96) under the heading "1985 Without Plan." However, these numbers do not always agree precisely with those given in the MacRae memorandum, apparently due to inadvertent errors. Thus in the *NEP* table, 0.9 MBD of "refinery gain" is added to the overall fuel supply; actually it should be *subtracted,* since "refinery gain" is fuel *consumed* by refineries during their operation. The figures in the *NEP* tables under the heading "1985 With Plan" represent the output of the altered PIES model for a new scenario, which includes the new policies that, if NEP was put into effect, would govern the 1985 energy budget.

page 16: CARTER QUOTATION: See *The New York Times,* April 19, 1977.

page 17: "A MATHEMATICAL FABRICATION": The origin of the information, cited in the text, regarding the deliberate alteration of the PIES model by the White House energy staff is of some interest. As noted in Chapter 1, soon after the National Energy Plan (NEP) was released in April 1977, it was apparent that there were puzzling discrepancies between the administration's claims about the Plan and the facts, as revealed by the numbers published in the *NEP* tables. Following David Freeman's comment that these numbers were not "worth talking about," I was particularly interested in knowing where they came from, and inquired among congressional energy staffs about the availability of descriptions of the mathematical model that was the presumed source of the numbers. I am grateful to Ms. Bethany Weidner of Senator James Abourezk's staff, who in response to my inquiry mentioned a complaint from the Texas Energy Advisory Council (TEAC), an official state agency, about the inaccessibility of the model that provided the Plan's data.

This led me to Mr. Milton L. Halloway, executive director of TEAC, who in July 1978 was kind enough to send me a remarkable document, which he had written for TEAC: "The National Energy Plan Analysis and the Texas Energy Advisory Council's Freedom of Information Request: Interpretations and Implications."

The TEAC report is a detailed account of TEAC's effort, beginning in June 1977, to obtain the data on which the Plan was based. TEAC wanted the tapes that constituted the model in order to compare the Plan's computations with the independent analyses that Governor Briscoe had asked TEAC and several Texas universities to carry out. Despite various promises, the information was not forthcoming from DOE, and on October 26, 1977, TEAC filed a formal request under the provisions of the Freedom of Information Act. Finally, according to the Holloway report, on December 5, 1977, TEAC "received a letter from DOE and a computer tape of the oil and gas supply models used in NEP analysis, but they were unusable." After complaining once more, on January 5, 1978, "TEAC received usable copy of oil and gas supply model, but without the required data set and without documentation."

Although TEAC was later able to piece together the needed information from the tapes, the report complains that "no up-to-date documentation exists for understanding and operating the model." The TEAC report then refers to the PART report, cited in the text, to show that major revisions were made in the model without documentation. The report concludes with the recommendation that "the Council [TEAC] encourage Congressional Conferees on Energy to cease discussions on the NEP until the task of an adequate, outside critique of the PIES model is complete." Had this advice been heeded, the Congress might have learned, in time to influence its action on it, that the Plan was based on gravely defective computations as a result of the changes that the White House staff had made in the PIES model.

I am grateful to Mr. Holloway for copies of the Christie/ Hall and MacRae memoranda, which I received, as well, from another source. Finally, in order to confirm the data in the MacRae memorandum, I asked for and received from DOE (on August 4, 1978), "the April 1977 PIES run for 1985 produced in support of the National Energy Plan analysis." This detailed computer printout confirmed the numbers cited in the MacRae memorandum.

Thus, contrary to the wishes of Congress, as clearly expressed in the Energy Conservation and Production Act, the White House staff breached the wall that Congress had intended to erect between the Office of Energy Information and Analysis, and the PIES model itself, and those who make policy and wield political power. Congress intended to protect the objectivity of energy information from those who might have the power to alter that information in their own interests. That the White House staff did even attempt to violate the integrity of the PIES model testifies to the importance of this protection; that the attempt succeeded suggests that the protection was inadequate.

In a world in which knowledge can be obscurely hidden in computer tapes, we need to be aware of the close, circular relation between knowledge and power. Knowledge *is* power, but only if it is exclusively held; power, as we have seen only too often (not only in this instance, but also in the shameful events of Watergate), can be used to corrupt knowledge, to hold information exclusively, to alter it in the service of power. When those in power succeed in corrupting information that is essential to judge what they plan to do with that power, democratic governance is frustrated. When the Carter administration breached the integrity of the government's energy information system, it went a long way toward crippling the democratic process by which the administration's Plan should have been judged.

3 THE NATIONAL ENERGY ACT: The Politics of Defeat

page 18: CARTER QUOTATION: See *The New York Times,* October 14, 1977. The quoted statement from *The New York Times* is in the same article.

page 18: CHANGE IN PUBLIC'S VIEW OF CARTER: See, for example, the article "The President, His Policy and Trust in Government," *The New York Times,* June 30, 1978.

page 18: CARTER'S NINETY-DAY DEADLINE: See his first presidential interview, *The New York Times,* January 25, 1977.

page 18: NATIONAL ENERGY ACT: The figures cited here refer to the version of the bill to "establish a comprehensive national energy policy," as submitted to Congress by the President, on April 29, 1977.

page 18: LEGISLATIVE HISTORY OF NATIONAL ENERGY ACT IN THE HOUSE: The overall history of the bill is described in *The New York Times,* May 4, 1977. The final marked-up version is reported in *The Energy Daily* 5 (137), July 15, 1977. Final House approval of HR 8444 is described in *The New York Times,* August 6, 1977, and in *The Energy Daily* 5 (155), August 10, 1977.

page 19: ANDERSON QUOTATION: See *The Energy Daily* 5 (140), July 20, 1977.

page 19: THE AD HOC COMMITTEE REPORT: *House Report,* 543, Vol. 1, 95th Congress, First Session, Ad Hoc Committee on Energy, Chairman Thomas L. Ashley, p. 5.

page 19: RIBICOFF QUOTATION: See *The New York Times,* October 6, 1977.

page 19: SENATE VOTE TO DEREGULATE NATURAL GAS: See *The New York Times,* October 4, 1977, and October 6, 1977.

page 20: SCHLESINGER'S GAS PRICE COMPROMISE AND CARTER'S DISAVOWAL: See *The New York Times,* November 22, 1977, and December 1, 1977.

page 20: SENATOR JACKSON'S ANNOUNCEMENT: See the Washington *Post,* April 24, 1978; the *Wall Street Journal,* April 22, 1978.

page 20: FAILURE TO ACHIEVE COMPROMISE IN AUGUST: See Washington *Post,* August 9, 1978; *Wall Street Journal,* August 9, 1978, and August 14, 1978.

page 20: ADMINISTRATION HORSE-TRADING ON THE COMPROMISE BILL: This is discussed in an informative article, "The Nuance of the Wink and the Nod," the Washington *Post,* August 26, 1978. See also related articles in the same issue of the Washington *Post.*

page 20: FINAL PASSAGE OF NATIONAL ENERGY ACT BY THE SENATE: See the Washington *Post,* October 16, 1978; the *Wall Street Journal,* October 16, 1978.

page 20: PROCEDURAL VOTE IN THE HOUSE: See the *Wall Street Journal,* October 16, 1978. The quotation is from this article. The procedural vote, which passed by one vote out of 415, determined the fate of the bill. The actual vote to approve the bill had a larger majority.

page 21: HARLEY STAGGERS AND TOBY MOFFETT QUOTATIONS: See the *Wall Street Journal* article cited above.

page 21: HERBLOCK CARTOON: The cartoon first appeared in the Washington *Post,* and was reprinted in *U.S. News & World Report,* October 23, 1978.

page 21: HISTORY OF FEDERAL CONTROLS ON GAS PRICES: For a helpful discussion of this rather complex subject, see Federal Power Commission, *National Gas Survey,* Vol. I, pp. 80–99 (Washington, D.C.: U.S. Government Printing Office, 1975).

page 21: CARTER LETTER TO BRISCOE: The letter is quoted in an article entitled "Carter Says His Aim Is an Eventual End to Gas Price Curbs," *The New York Times,* October 29, 1977.

page 21: CARTER QUOTATION: See *The New York Times* article cited above.

page 21: ASHLEY QUOTATION: See *The New York Times* article cited above.

page 21: GAS PRICES UNDER NATIONAL ENERGY ACT: For a discussion of the structure and the expected effect of the gas bill, see *The New York Times,* November 18, 1978.

page 22: CARTER QUOTATION: These statements were made during the course of an extensive, wide-ranging interview with six editors of *U.S. News & World Report.* See *U.S. News & World Report,* August 21, 1978.

4 THE ECONOMICS OF ENERGY: The Politics of Inflation

page 24: HENRY KISSINGER'S PARTICIPATION IN CITIZENS' ALLIANCE TO SAVE ENERGY: See *The New York Times,* April 25, 1977.

page 24: CARTER QUOTATION: President Carter's complaint was voiced in an interview with editors and directors of *The New York Times* on July 30, 1977. See *The New York Times,* August 14, 1977.

page 24: GALLUP POLL OF APRIL 1977: See *The New York Times,* April 15, 1977.

page 24: GALLUP POLL OF JULY 1977: See *The New York Times,* August 14, 1977.

page 24: FERRELL QUOTATION: Contained in the verbatim account of the Charleston meeting. See Office of the White House Press Secretary (Charleston, West Virginia), "Remarks of the President and Question and Answer Session at the Energy Roundtable Conference" (Washington, D.C.: The White House, March 17, 1977), p. 9.

page 24: HALL QUOTATION: Contained in the verbatim account of the Detroit meeting. See Office of the White House Press Secretary (Detroit, Michigan), "Remarks of the President and Question and Answer Session at the Community Services Administration Public Policy Forum (Washington, D.C.: The White House, October 21, 1977), p. 3. In replying to Mr. Hall, Mr. Carter said: "Very good statement," whereupon the audience applauded. The President then talked about a meeting with steel executives and labor leaders in which the depressed state of the industry was discussed. He concluded his reply by remarking: "I think the passage of a new energy bill . . . will provide increasing demands for steel." There was no applause. A more cogent comment about the relation of the steel industry to the energy crisis might have dealt with the fact that the industry produces a great deal of waste heat, which, through cogeneration, could be used to meet the growing demand for electricity. Steel mills do use cogeneration to produce power for their own use, but that generally makes use of only about half of the available heat. In cities like Cleveland, Ohio, and Gary, Indiana, where there are a number of steel mills, linking the steel mills into the cities' power systems could keep utility rates down and help the steel industry as well.

page 24: CARTER QUOTATION: From the President's news conference of December 12, 1978, as reported in the *Weekly Compilation of Presidential Documents,* December 18, 1978.

page 25: NPC STUDY: A preliminary version of this study appeared in 1971, and final reports were published in 1972 and 1973. For the preliminary report, see *U.S. Energy Outlook, An Initial Appraisal 1971–85* (Washington, D.C.: National Petroleum Council, July 15, 1971). The final reports deal, in considerable detail, with the prospects for producing and using various fuels.

page 25: OIL PRICES: See *U.S. Energy Outlook: Oil and Gas Availability* (Washington, D.C.: National Petroleum Council, 1973), p. 718. This is the most important of the detailed "U.S. Energy Outlook Reports." Price increases quoted are in 1970 constant dollars, given a constant 15 percent rate of return on net fixed assets for the lower forty-eight states and south Alaska, which corresponds to NPC Case IA (low finding rate).

page 25: KNEE-DEEP IN TELEVISION SETS: The annual sales of television sets in the U.S. from 1947 to 1957 were obtained from *Business Statistics, 1975 Biennial Survey* (Washington, D.C.: Bureau of Economic Analysis, U.S. Department of Commerce, 1976), p. 161, and the trend in sales of sets to 2000 was extrapolated from these data. The extrapolated curve predicts the production of enough television sets by 2000 to cover the entire surface of the United States with them.

page 27: "WHEN EXPLOITATION OF THE U.S. OIL RESOURCE BEGAN IN EARNEST": For the relevant figures, see *Petroleum Facts & Figures,* 1971 edition (Washington, D.C.: American Petroleum Institute, 1971), pp. 68–71.

page 27: THE PRICE OF BUFFALO ROBES: For the relevant figures, see Barry Commoner, "The Need for an Energy Policy," presented at the Fourth Annual Illinois Energy Conference on Illinois Coal, September 16–17, 1976, p. 11.

page 28: OPEC OIL PRICES: The prices quoted are the posted values for Arabian light 34° gravity crude oil, FOB Ras Tanura in current dollars per barrel. See Foster Associates, *Energy Prices 1960–73* (Cambridge, Mass.: Ballinger Publishing Company, 1974), p. 18.

page 28: BLAIR QUOTATION: John M. Blair, *The Control of Oil* (New York: Pantheon Books, 1976), p. 275. This remarkable book by a remarkable man is essential to an understanding of how the U.S. oil companies have so successfully manipulated the world-wide economics of this resource.

page 28: THE OPEC OIL MINISTERS' RESPONSE: The point being made here is that the OPEC oil ministers must have known from the NPC report "U.S. Energy Outlook," as early as 1971, that the U.S. oil industry predicted that although prices for domestic U.S. oil had been essentially constant for about twenty-five years, they would begin to rise exponentially after 1972. It is inconceivable that, thus informed, the OPEC countries would fail to raise their own price accordingly. In this sense it is the NPC report that triggered the subsequent escalation of oil prices. Between 1950 and 1973 the price of domestic oil did not have to rise because it was well above the cost curve. It is probable that the reason the industry produced the NPC report at the time it did was that the cost curve, which had been rising along an exponential course, was bound to reach the fixed price in the 1970–73 period, so that the industry had to raise prices thereafter to maintain profits, and needed to explain why this was so.

page 28: INCREASED TARGET RATES OF PROFIT: Blair, pp. 304–305.

page 28: PREDICTED VERSUS ACTUAL 1978 OIL PRICES: The data are from *U.S. Energy Outlook: Oil and Gas Availability;* implicit price deflators from *Business Statistics, 1975,* and *Survey of Current Business* (U.S. Department of Commerce, Bureau of Economic Analysis) (Washington, D.C.: U.S. Government Printing Office, 1976, 1978), were used to convert current dollars into constant 1978 dollars. For the actual current price of domestic oil, see *Monthly Energy Review,* January 1979 (cited above), p. 71. For a discussion of the relation between oil prices and production, and between oil prices and inflation, see Barry Commoner, testimony before the Environment, Energy and Natural Resources Subcommittee of the House Committee on Government Operations in hearings on "The Administration's Solar Energy Policy," June 13, 1978 (Washington, D.C.: U.S. Government Printing Office, 1979).

page 28: WHOLESALE COMMODITY PRICES: The most convenient places to find these data are: *Business Statistics, 1975* (cited above), and monthly issues of the *Survey of Current Business,* a journal published by the U.S. Department of Congress.

page 28: *Wall Street Journal* QUOTATION: From an article in the *Wall Street Journal,* April 7, 1977. Their comments on inflation have become more somber since then.

page 29: EFFECT OF ENERGY PRICES ON THE POOR: See Federal Energy Administration, *Report to Congress on the Economic Impact of Energy Actions as Required by Public Law 93-275, Section 18(D)* (Washington, D.C.: U.S. Government Printing Office, July 1975). FEA/b-76/376.

page 29: ENERGY PRICES: The cited figures refer to the wholesale price index for fuel and power, as published in *Business Statistics, 1975* and *Survey of Current Business* (both cited above).

page 29: COMPLAINTS FROM THE BUSINESS COMMUNITY: Numerous examples could be cited. For typical ones, see the *Wall Street Journal,* April 4, 1977, and *Business Week,* September 22, 1975 (p. 42).

page 30: ENERGY INDUSTRY'S DEMAND FOR CAPITAL: See Bankers Trust Company, *U.S. Energy and Capital* (New York: Bankers Trust Company, Energy Group, 1978), p. 28.

page 30: CAPITAL REQUIRED FOR OIL AND GAS PRODUCTION: Ibid., pp. 12, 17.

page 30: FEA STUDY: See *Project Independence Blueprint Final Task Force Report on Oil: Possible Levels of Future Production* (values for capital productivity were computed from the data on pp. IV-2 and IV-21). See Barry Commoner, *The Poverty of Power* (New York: Alfred A. Knopf, 1976), pp. 53–54, for a discussion of the capital productivity of oil production, also based on the FEA report.

page 30: AMERICAN GAS ASSOCIATION STUDY: See *A Comparison of Capital Investment Requirements for Alternative Domestic Energy Supplies,* cited above.

page 30: UNEMPLOYMENT AMONG YOUNG PEOPLE: See *Monthly Labor Review,* October 1978, p. 70, and *Handbook of Labor Statistics 1977,* Bureau of Labor Statistics Bulletin 1955 (Washington, D.C.: U.S. Government Printing Office, 1978).

page 30: CAPITAL REQUIREMENTS FOR COAL CONVERSION: The figure cited is from *The National Energy Plan,* cited above. During subsequent discussions in Congress and elsewhere, estimates ranging up to $80 billion have been made.

5 SOLAR VERSUS NUCLEAR ENERGY: The Politics of Choice

page 32: THE ROLES OF NUCLEAR AND SOLAR ENERGY IN THE NATIONAL ENERGY PLAN: See Barry Commoner, "The National Energy Plan: A Critique," presented at the National League of Cities Task Force on Energy Meeting, May 10, 1979, for computations based on the data published in *The National Energy Plan,* which evaluate the relative contributions of different sources of energy, and of conservation, to the Plan. See also Barry Commoner, "Solar Energy, Myths and Motives," *Hospital Practice,* February 1977, p. 53.

page 33: NELSON QUOTATION: "Energy Research and Development and Small Business," Hearings before the Select Committee on Small Business of the United States Senate. Part 1, May 13 and 14, 1975 (Washington, D.C.: U.S. Government Printing Office, 1975), p. 3. See also Parts 2 and 3 of the hearings, held on October 8, 22, November 18, 1975, and May 23, 1977.

page 33: "STATEMENT OF DONALD B. CRAVEN . . .": See Hearings, cited above, Part 1, p. 413.

page 33: "THE PRESENT ENERGY SITUATION . . .": See Hearings, cited above, Part 1, p. 417.

page 33: "ACCELERATED USE OF SOLAR ENERGY . . .": See Hearings, cited above, Part 1, pp. 422–423.

page 33: "WE ARE DEVELOPING . . .": See Hearings, cited above, Part 1, p. 423.

page 33: STATEMENTS BY HATHAWAY, CRAVEN, AND KUHN: See Hearings, cited above, Part 1, p. 460.

page 33: FUNDS FOR SOLAR ENERGY: See Hearings, cited above, Part 1, p. 630.

page 33: FEDERAL BUDGET FOR NUCLEAR POWER: See U.S. Department of Commerce, Bureau of the Census, *Statistical Abstract of the United States 1976 (Statistical Abstract)* (Washington, D.C.: U.S. Government Printing Office, 1977), p. 564.

page 34: SECTION 110 OF THE ACT: See EPCA, Public Law 94-385, 94th Congress, H.R. 12169, August 14, 1976, printed version of the bill (Washington, D.C.: U.S. Government Printing Office, 1976).

page 35: COST OF PHOTOVOLTAIC CELLS IN 1976: See Federal Energy Administration, Task Force on Solar Energy Commercialization, "Preliminary Analysis of an Option for the Federal Photovoltaic Utilization Program" (Washington, D.C.: Federal Energy Administration, July 20, 1977), p. 3.

page 35: COST OF POWER FROM DRY CELLS: See R. M. Winegarner, "Near Term Uses for Terrestrial Photovoltaics," in the *Proceedings of the 1977 Annual Meeting of the American Section of the International Solar Energy Society* (Cape Canaveral, Fla.: American Section of the International Solar Energy Society, June 1977), pp. 28-10 to 28-12.

page 35: GENERATOR SET PRICES: See "Preliminary Analysis of an Option for the Federal Photovoltaic Utilization Program," cited above. This is also the source for the figure for photovoltaic cell production in 1976.

page 35: PRODUCTION EXPERIENCE IN THE INTEGRATED-CIRCUITS INDUSTRY: "DOD Photovoltaic Energy Systems Market Inventory and Analysis" (2 vols.) (Washington, D.C.: Federal Energy Administration, June 1977 and August 1977), vol. 1, pp. ix10–ix11.

page 36: SURVEY OF DOD GENERATOR SETS: See "Preliminary Analysis," pp. 4–8, and "DOD Photovoltaic Energy Systems Market Inventory and Analysis." The cost of operating these sets did not include the installation (capital) cost for the engines which would be used for back-up power supply.

page 36: BREAK-EVEN COSTS OF PHOTOVOLTAIC CELLS: See "Preliminary Analysis," p. 9.

page 36: THE COST AND SAVINGS OF A 152 MW PURCHASE PROGRAM: See "Preliminary Analysis," p. 1.

page 36: REMOTE POWER APPLICATIONS OF PHOTOVOLTAICS: See BDM Corporation, "An Analysis of the Potential Industry / Market Impacts of the Federal Photovoltaic Utilization Program (FPUP)," Submitted to the Department of Energy (Federal Energy Administration Task Force on Solar Energy Commercialization, prepared under purchase order 05-77-5731-0, October 27, 1977 (BDM/W-77-486-TR), p. 9.

page 36: POTENTIAL MARKET FOR PHOTOVOLTAIC CELLS: See "Preliminary Analysis," p. 33.

page 37: NEW SILICON-SLICING TECHNIQUE: See FPUP, cited above, pp. 22–23.

page 38: NATIONAL ENERGY PLAN QUOTATION: See *The National Energy Plan,* cited above, p. 76.

page 38: PASSAGE OF A FEDERAL PHOTOVOLTAIC PURCHASE PLAN: See H.R. 12874, "The Solar Photovoltaic Energy Research, Development, and Demonstration Act of 1978," signed by the President on November 6, 1978. This bill was included in the package of bills approved by Congress as the National Energy Act.

page 38: EFFECT OF THE $98 MILLION PURCHASE PLAN: See FPUP, cited above.

page 38: WINDMILLS: The figures are cited from The Metrek Division of The Mitre Corporation, "Executive Summary of the Preliminary Federal Commercialization Plan for Wind Energy Conversion Systems," prepared for the Federal Energy Administration Task Force on Solar Energy Commercialization (McLean, Va.: The Mitre Corporation, January 1977), MTR-7365, p. S 30. See also Julian McCall, "Windmills," *Environment* 15 (1), January/February 1973, pp. 6–17, and David Rittenhouse Inglis, *Wind Power and Other Energy Options* (Ann Arbor, Mich.: University of Michigan Press, 1978), pp. 44–69.

page 38: WIND/ELECTRIC GENERATORS AT PUMPED STORAGE SITES: See C. J. Todd et al., "Cost Effective Electric Power Generation from the Wind: A System Linking Windpower with Hydroelectric Storage and Long-Distance Transmission" (Denver: U.S. Department of the Interior, Bureau of Reclamation, August 1977), p. 25.

page 39: STUDIES OF SOLAR HEATING: For the CBNS study, see Ali Shams and Rudi Fichtenbaum, "The Feasibility of Solar House Heating: A Study in Applied Economics" (St. Louis, Mo.: Center for the Biology of Natural Systems, April 1976). For the NSF study, see Arthur E. McGarity, "Solar Heating and Cooling: An Economic Assessment," prepared for the National Science Foundation, Directorate of Scientific, Technological and International Affairs (Washington, D.C.: U.S. Government Printing Office, 1977). Stock No. 038-000-00300-3. For the study for the Joint Economic Committee, see William D. Shulze et al., "The Economics of Solar Home Heating" (Washington, D.C.: U.S. Government Printing Office, March 13, 1977). For the ERDA study, see Energy Research and Development Administration, Division of Solar Energy, "An Economic Analysis of Solar Water and Space Heating" (Washington, D.C.: U.S. Government Printing Office, November 1976) (prepared for ERDA by The Mitre Corporation).

page 39: RECENT DOE STUDY: See Roger H. Bezdek, "An Analysis of the Current Economic Feasibility of Solar Water and Space Heating," prepared for the U.S. Department of Energy, Assistant Secretary for Conservation and Solar Applications (Washington, D.C.: U.S. Government Printing Office, 1978). DOE/CS-0023.

page 40: STATE-BY-STATE ANALYSIS OF SOLAR HEATING: See Shulze et al., cited above.

page 40: MARKET FOR RESIDENTIAL HEATING: For an analysis of the effect of expanded output of solar collectors on price, see The Mitre Corporation Study, "Systems Descriptions and Engineering Costs for Solar Related Technologies," Vol. 1, Appendix (Mitre Report No. MTR-7485) (McLean, Va.: The Mitre Corporation, 1977), as reported in "Solar Energy, A Comparative Analysis to the Year 2020," by G. Bennington et al. (Mitre Report No. MTR-7579) (McLean, Va.: The Mitre Corporation, March 1978), p. 12.

page 40: OTA STUDY: See Congress of the U.S., Office of Technology Assessment, *Application of Solar Technology to Today's Energy Needs,* Vol. I (June 1978), Vol. II (September 1978) (Washington, D.C.: U.S. Government Printing Office, 1978). USGPO stock numbers, Vol. I: 052-003-00539-5; Vol. II: 052-003-00608-1.

page 41: SIMPLE METHANE GENERATORS: See, for example, V. Smil, "Energy Solution in China," *Environment* 19 (7), October 1977, pp. 29–31.

page 41: SCHLESINGER QUOTATION: See *The Energy Daily* 6 (218), November 13, 1978, p. 3.

page 41: FARMERS AND SOLAR ENERGY: For a general discussion, see Barry Commoner, "Energy and Rural America," paper presented at the Third National Conference on Rural America, Washington, D.C.; December 5, 1977 (St. Louis, Mo.: CBNS, 1979).

page 41: ARCHIE ZEITHAMER'S ALCOHOL PLANT: The information cited here was supplied by Mr. Zeithamer to David Freedman, a member of the CBNS staff who visited the plant in November 1978.

page 41: LEN SCHIEFFER'S METHANE GENERATOR: See Tom Abeles, David Freedman, David Ellsworth, and Luc DeBaere, "Energy and Economic Assessment of Anaerobic Digesters for Rural Waste Management," prepared for the U.S. Environmental Protection Agency (Contract No. R-804-457-010) (Rice Lake, Wisc.: University of Wisconsin Center–Barron County, June 1978).

page 41: TED LANDERS'S METHANE SYSTEM: The information cited here was supplied by Mr. Landers in a telephone conversation with David Freedman of the CBNS staff in December 1978.

page 41: ALCOHOL PRODUCTION IN MISSOURI, ILLINOIS, COLORADO, AND BRAZIL: See R. Carlson, B. Commoner, D. Freedman, and R. Scott, "Studies on the Economic Potential of On-Farm

Energy Production Systems: Interim Report on Possible Energy-Production Alternatives in Crop/Livestock Agriculture" (St. Louis, Mo.: Center for the Biology of Natural Systems, January 4, 1979).

page 42: COUNCIL ON ENVIRONMENTAL QUALITY REPORT: See "Solar Energy: Progress and Promise" (Washington, D.C.: U.S. Government Printing Office, April 1978).

page 42: ENERGY CONTENT OF GRAIN AND HAY: Computed from statistics contained in "Studies on the Economic Potential of On-Farm Energy Production Systems," cited above. Total production of grain, soybeans, silage, hay, and pasture was 442 million tons in 1974, which, if burned, would generate roughly 7 quadrillion BTU. About 13 percent of U.S. arable land was not harvested in 1974, and therefore the maximum production without any land idle in that year would have been about 8 quads.

page 42: CBNS SCHEME FOR AGRICULTURAL ENERGY PRODUCTION: The reasoning and data that lead to the conclusion that it might be possible to produce significant amounts of energy from agriculture without reducing food production are described in Carlson et al., cited above. At present, agriculture is a *net consumer* of about 2 quads of energy annually. The CBNS scheme would involve using an additional 1 quad of energy, but it would *produce* 9 quads of energy (computed in terms of the conventional fuel that it could replace). Thus the scheme would convert agriculture from a net consumer of 2 quads of energy to a net producer of 8 quads of energy. At a time when vehicular fuel is in short supply, even for farm equipment, and farmers are forced to pay ever higher prices for it, it would make a great deal of sense to develop on-farm energy production. Many farms and increasing numbers of legislators are interested in such a program, but as of March 1978, the government has taken no significant steps in that direction.

page 43: METHANE FROM KELP: See Howard V. Wilcox, "The Ocean Energy and Food Farm Project," paper presented at the Washington Conference on Bioconversion, Shoreham-Americana Hotel, Washington, D.C., March 10, 1976 (manuscript available from the Naval Undersea Center, San Diego, California). See also Robert Hodam, "Energy from Kelp," a staff analysis for the Energy Resources Conservation and Development Commission (Sacramento, Cal.: ERCDC, August 15, 1977); manuscript kindly supplied by Dr. Hodam.

page 43: GASOHOL COMPETITIVE WITH HIGH-TEST GASOLINE: The relevant data and computations are given in Carlson et al., cited above. There seems to be a good deal of misunderstanding about this situation at present, based on the simple notion that alcohol costing $1.00 per gallon cannot compete with gasoline that costs $.70 or so per gallon. Once again, we see here an example of the fact that if it is to be economically effective, solar energy must be carefully integrated into the energy-using system.

page 44: THE AMERICAN PHYSICAL SOCIETY REPORT ON PHOTOVOLTAIC ENERGY CONVERSION: See H. Ehrenreich, Chairman, *Principle Conclusions of the American Physical Society Study Group on Solar Photovoltaic Energy Conversion* (New York: The American Physical Society, January 1979).

page 44: THE CENTRALIZED SOLAR PLANT AT BARSTOW, CALIFORNIA: For a brief discussion of this DOE project, see *The New York Times,* November 13, 1977.

page 45: JOINT VENTURE BETWEEN SOLAREX AND MONTEDISON CORPORATIONS: See the *Solar Energy Intelligence Report,* 4 (48), November 27, 1978, p. 367.

page 45: PRESENT U.S. PRODUCTION OF PHOTOVOLTAIC CELLS: See the report of the . . . *Study Group on Solar Photovoltaic Energy Conversion,* cited above. p. 21.

page 45: U.S. OIL DEFICIT CAUSED BY THE CUTBACK IN IRANIAN PRODUCTION: See, for example, the *Wall Street Journal,* February 13, 1979.

page 45: *Solar Energy Intelligence Report* QUOTATION: See *Solar Energy Intelligence Report,* 4 (12), March 20, 1978, p. 77.

page 45: O'LEARY QUOTATION: See St. Louis *Post-Dispatch,* November 29, 1977.

page 45: ATOMIC INDUSTRIAL FORUM DATA ON THE COST OF NUCLEAR POWER: The conclusion cited here was computed from AIF data in B. Commoner and R. Scott, "Testimony Submitted to the Subcommittee on Environment, Energy and Natural Resources of the U.S. House of Representatives Committee on Governmental Operations on the Cost of Nuclear Power," October 14, 1977 (Washington, D.C.: U.S. Government Printing Office, 1978).

page 45: FALLING ORDERS FOR NUCLEAR PLANTS: See R. W. McCoy, Jr., "Electric Utility Generating Equipment, Status Report on Worldwide Nuclear Reactors as of December 31, 1977" (New York: Kidder Peabody & Co., May 3, 1978).

page 45: REACTOR ORDERS IN 1978: See *The Energy Daily* 6 (244), December 21, 1978, p. 1.

page 45: NUCLEAR POWER GENERATION IN 1975: See *Monthly Energy Review,* November 1978, p. 54.

page 45: AEC PROJECTIONS OF NUCLEAR POWER CAPACITY: See U.S. Atomic Energy Commission, *The Nuclear Industry 1973,* WASH 1174–73 (Washington, D.C.: U.S. Government Printing Office, 1973).

page 46: MILLER QUOTATION: Saunders Miller, *The Economics of Nuclear and Coal Power* (New York: Praeger Publishers, 1976), p. 109. This book is a careful analysis of the problem that ought to be required reading for every utility executive.

page 46: THE COST OF NUCLEAR POWER PLANTS: For a general discussion of the reasons for the unexpected high cost of nuclear power, see Barry Commoner and Hans Bethe, "A Public Debate on Nuclear Energy," *Cornell Review,* Spring 1977.

page 46: GE POSSIBLY CLOSING ITS REACTOR DIVISION: See *The New York Times,* May 15, 1977.

page 46: *Wall Street Journal* ARTICLE ON GE: See the *Wall Street Journal,* September 27, 1977.

page 46: CARTER QUOTATION: Given that the administration has been pressing for the rapid development of nuclear power, this statement is frequently cited by Mr. Carter's disappointed supporters. See, for example, the record of Carter's first election debate on September 23, 1976, as reported in *President Carter* (Washington, D.C.: Congressional Quarterly, Inc., April 1977). For a reiteration of this position, see the National Energy Plan (NEP), cited above.

page 46: PRESIDENT CARTER'S STATEMENT ON NUCLEAR POWER IN THE ABSENCE OF REPORTERS: See *Nuclear Industry,* May 1978, pp. 6–7. The occasion was an interesting one. On April 13, 1978, the AFL-CIO Building and Construction Trades Department and the National Constructors Association (which represents contractors who build nuclear power plants) signed an agreement designed to speed construction and "place the nuclear plants on line sooner." The agreement includes a no-strike provision, which, in the words of a memorandum from Secretary Schlesinger to Mr. Carter, led the AFL-CIO department to be "concerned about the effect of the agreement on its local unions." The President was urged to participate in a White House ceremony at which the agreement would be signed in order to "drape ourselves in the flag," as one union source quoted by the *Wall Street Journal* (April 19, 1978) put it. According to the account of the ceremony in *Nuclear Industry:*

One industry participant at the White House ceremony observed that after the picture-taking was over, President Carter shooed the photographers and newsmen out and then emphasized to his union-management guests that the light water reactor [the conventional nuclear power plant] was a vital segment of the nation's energy picture.

"I found myself wondering, why didn't he put that kind of emphasis on light water reactors when the press was there?" he said.

page 46: SCHLESINGER QUOTATION: Speech by James R. Schlesinger to the Meeting of the Governing Board of the International Energy Act at the Ministerial Level, October 5, 1977; manuscript obtained from the press office of the U.S. Department of Energy, p. 7. Environmentalists who support the administration sometimes take the position that while Schlesinger is "for" nuclear power, Mr. Carter is "against" it, but it is never made clear why such a basic disagreement, if it exists, should be tolerated by the President.

page 46: ROLE OF NUCLEAR POWER IN NATIONAL ENERGY PLAN: See Commoner, *The National Energy Plan: A Critique,* cited above.

page 46: DEVELOPMENTS IN THE U.S. ANTI-NUCLEAR MOVEMENT: See *The Critical Mass Journal,* June 1977, September 1977, and July 1978.

page 46: STATE BANS ON CONSTRUCTION OF NEW NUCLEAR PLANTS: See Washington *Post,* August 19, 1978, and *The Energy Daily* 6 (217), November 9, 1978.

page 46: THE ROLE OF THE NUCLEAR ISSUE IN SWEDISH POLITICS: See *Business Week,* September 11, 1978, pp. 69–70.

page 46: THE NUCLEAR ISSUE IN FRANCE: See *The New York Times,* August 2, 1977.

page 46: THE NUCLEAR ISSUE IN WEST GERMANY: See *The New York Times,* August 2, 1977, and December 3, 1978.

page 46: THE NUCLEAR ISSUE IN SPAIN: See *The New York Times,* July 16, 1977.

page 46: THE NUCLEAR ISSUE IN ITALY: See *The New York Times,* August 2, 1977.

page 46: THE NUCLEAR ISSUE IN AUSTRIA: See St. Louis *Post-Dispatch,* November 6, 1978.

page 47: THE NUCLEAR ISSUE IN IRAN: See *The Energy Daily* 6 (198), October 13, 1978, p. 1.

page 47: THREE MILE ISLAND NUCLEAR POWER PLANT: Factual material is from press reports during the period of the accident. See, in particular, *The New York Times*, April 16, 1979.

page 48: URANIUM SUPPLIES: See *Nuclear Fuel Cycle,* Energy Research and Development Administration, Document ERDA-33 (Washington, D.C.: U.S. Government Printing Office, 1975).

6 THE SOLAR TRANSITION: The Politics of Transformation

page 49: THE EFFICIENCY OF ENERGY USE IN THE U.S.: See *Efficient Use of Energy, APS Studies on the Technical Aspects of the More Efficient Use of Energy,* edited by K. W. Ford et al. (New York: American Institute of Physics, 1975), pp. 4, 32, 35. This subject and the importance of the Ford report are discussed in *The Poverty of Power* (cited above), pp. 6–38.

page 49: THE SOLAR TRANSITION: The material presented in this chapter is discussed in more detail in the following places: Barry Commoner, "The Solar Transition," *Environment,* April 1978, p. 6 (a paper presented the Solar Energy Symposium of the Federal Trade Commission, Washington, D.C., December 15, 1977). See also Barry Commoner, testimony before Subcommittee on Environment, Energy and Natural Resources of the Government Operations Committee, June 13, 1978 (cited above in the note for p. 28).

page 50: THE CAPITAL PRODUCTIVITY OF ENERGY PRODUCTION: The statement is based on an analysis of capital investment presented in B. Bosworth et al., *Capital Needs in the Seventies* (Washington, D.C.: Brookings Institution, 1975), pp. 27–79, and on energy production figures reported in the U.S. Department of the Interior publication *Energy Perspectives* (Washington, D.C.: U.S. Government Printing Office, February 1975). For a further discussion of this issue, see *The Poverty of Power* (cited above), pp. 200–202.

page 50: THE SHARE OF BUSINESS CAPITAL THAT WILL BE REQUIRED FOR ENERGY PRODUCTION: See *U.S. Energy and Capital,* cited above.

page 50: THE RELATIVE VOLUMES OF NATURAL GAS AND JET FUEL: One cubic foot of jet fuel would contain about 7.5 gallons of fuel, which would have an energy content of about 960,000 BTU. In comparison, a cubic foot of natural gas at sea-level pressure contains about 1025 BTU, roughly $\frac{1}{1000}$ of the amount of energy in the cubic foot of jet fuel. A gaseous fuel can be compressed to a liquid with much smaller volume, but then it must be stored in very heavy tanks. It would be conceivable, but probably very inefficient, to operate an airplane on liquefied propane. The conversion factors are from the CRC *Handbook of Chemistry and Physics* (Cleveland, Ohio: The Chemical Rubber Publishing Company, 1963).

page 50: RELATIVE WEIGHTS OF JET FUEL AND BATTERIES: One cubic foot of jet fuel, containing 960,000 BTU, would weigh about 45 pounds, which would equal 21,000 BTU per pound of fuel. An ordinary auto battery will store about 1 kilowatt-hour of electricity, and will weigh about 50 pounds, which corresponds to about 70 BTU per pound, or $\frac{1}{300}$ of the amount of energy in a pound of jet fuel.

page 50: THE ENERGY EFFICIENCY OF MOTORS AND POWER PLANTS: See *Efficient Use of Energy . . . ,* cited above.

page 51: TRANSMISSION LOSSES IN THE U.S. POWER NETWORK: The figure cited is computed from the difference between the amount of electric power generated in the U.S. and the amount sold to ultimate customers. According to the *Statistical Abstract, 1976* (cited above), p. 616, power generation in 1975 amounted to 1,918 billion kWh, and total sales were 9.6 percent less (1,733 billion kWh).

page 51: THE COST OF DELIVERING VARIOUS FORMS OF ENERGY: See U.S. Congress, Office of Technology Assessment, *Application of Solar Technology to Today's Energy Needs* (cited above), Vol. I, p. 140.

page 52: "VERY FEW TAKERS": Apparently, only one U.S. nuclear power plant is designed to make use of its waste heat, by supplying it to the Dow Chemical Company's plant at Midland, Michigan. However, there are difficulties in licensing the plant thus far.

page 52: A RECENT PROPOSAL FOR A BREEDER-BASED POWER SYSTEM: See C. L. Rickard and R. C. Dahlberg, "Nuclear Power: A Balanced Approach," *Science,* 202:10 (November 1978), pp. 581–584. This article proposes a mixed thorium/uranium fuel cycle, of the type that seems to be favored by the Carter administration. The proposal envisages a country populated by some 400 nuclear breeders and advanced converter reactors (a hybrid between a conventional and a breeder reactor) in the year 2000, generating 400 billion watts, rising to 1000 plants, generating 1000 billion watts, in the year 2040. The cost of these plants (in constant 1976 dollars) was estimated from projections made by William E. Mooz, *Cost Analysis of Light Water Reactor Power Plants,* R-2304-DOE (Santa Monica, Cal.: Rand Corporation, June 1978). The Mooz report estimated that the cost of nuclear plants could rise to $3,417/kWh by 1990. At that rate, each plant, with a capacity of 1000 million watts, would cost $3.4 billion, and the entire 1000-plant system would cost $3.4 trillion. This does not include the cost of replacing plants that would wear out between now and 2040.

page 52: THE PRESENT NUCLEAR POWER SYSTEM: The number of operating nuclear power plants in the U.S. and their total capacity is reported in the *Monthly Energy Review,* November 1978, pp. 53–54. The average cost of these units was calculated from data given in the Mooz *Cost Analysis of Light Water Reactor Power Plants,* cited above.

page 52: THE EFFICIENCY OF ELECTRIC HEAT PUMPS: On the average, most heat pumps, which extract heat from outside air to warm inside space (air-to-air heat pumps), can produce significantly more energy than they consume. However, Professor Kurt H. Hohenemser of the Washington University School of Engineering, who has a sharp eye for these matters, points out that in cold weather, air-to-air heat pumps are ineffective and switch to electric resistance heat. Thus their overall efficiency, taking the entire heating season into account, may be rather low. Heat pumps that extract energy from underground water might avoid this problem.

page 53: QUOTATION FROM THE NRC MEETINGS: See *The New York Times,* April 13, 1979.

page 54: A RECENT COMPARISON OF THE SAFETY OF TWO NUCLEAR FUEL SYSTEMS: See R. C. Dahlberg, "Weapons Proliferation and Criteria for Evaluating Nuclear Fuel Cycles," *Bulletin of the Atomic Scientists,* 34 (1), January 1978, pp. 38–42.

page 54: BARTON QUOTATION: J. H. Barton, "Intensified Nuclear Safeguards and Civil Liberties," a paper prepared under Nuclear Regulatory Commission Contract No. AT(49-24)-0190. The paper was presented at a NRC-sponsored working conference on the Impact of Intensified Nuclear Safeguards on Civil Liberties, held at the Stanford University Law School, October 17–18, 1975. Unpublished manuscript.

page 54: ENERGY FROM CATTAILS IN MINNESOTA: The estimate was made by Roger G. Aiken of the University of Minnesota Center for the Study of the Physical Environment, as part of a very informative study of the state's energy resources, under the general title "Minnesota Alternative Energy Research and Development Policy Formulation Project," and reported to the Minnesota Energy Agency. The study is a good example of how solar energy needs to be carefully integrated into the local system of energy production and use. Energy consumption in the state was 1.15 quadrillion BTU (quads) in 1976; the total energy available from cattails was 3.175 quads, and from peat, 1.65 quads.

page 54: ENERGY FROM REEDS IN SWEDEN: See *Ambio,* VII (4), 1978, pp. 150–156.

page 54: ENERGY FROM SEWAGE, GARBAGE, AND WASTE PAPER: See L. L. Anderson, "Energy Potential from Organic Wastes: A Review of the Quantities and Sources," Bureau of Mine Information Circular 8549 (Washington, D.C.: U.S. Government Printing Office, 1972). This paper demonstrates that about 185 million tons of organic waste are produced each year in the forms of urban refuse (garbage, paper, and trash), industrial waste, and municipal sewage solids, which could be converted into about 1.9 trillion cubic feet (TCF) of methane, if collected and converted. This would be about 10 percent of 1977 U.S. consumption of natural gas, 19.6 TCF (see *Statistical Abstract,* 1978 [Washington, D.C.: U.S. Government Printing Office, 1979]).

page 55: FUELS FOR AIRPLANES: In theory, airplanes can use solid fuels that are very concentrated, in terms of energy content per pound (for example, solid fuels of the sort that drive missiles), or gaseous fuels stored in a solid material (such as hydrogen gas stored in a metal hydride), but no such technology appears to be feasible, at least in the near future. Hence, the discussion here centers on alternative liquid fuels.

page 55: ENERGY USE IN AIR AND GROUND TRANSPORTATION: See *End Use Energy Consumption Data Base: Series 1 Tables* (cited above), pp. 20, 36–37.

page 56: THE FIAT COGENERATOR: Engineering specifications for the unit are given in F. P. Ausiello et al., *TOTEM Total Energy Module* (Milan, Italy: Fiat Auto Group, September 1977). The TOTEM unit is a good example of the existing opportunities for making real improvements in the efficiency with which energy is used. The only cogenerators manufactured in the United States are large units, suitable for use in industry, or in large housing developments. TOTEM opens up opportunities for using cogeneration in the most common types of residences: single-family homes and relatively small multiple-family dwellings. It is also a good example of the economic stimulation that would result from the adoption of such sensible energy systems. While Fiat is reported to be building a new plant capable of producing some 50,000 units per year in Italy, there is no sign of interest as yet on the part of the U.S. automobile industry, which could certainly make good use of its idle capacity in this way. Some city officials have shown interest in using such cogenerators in urban redevelopment, notably in Los Angeles and in Gary, Indiana.

page 56: MIXING HYDROGEN WITH PIPELINE METHANE GAS: See C. R. Guerra et al., "Natural Gas Supplementation with Hydrogen," in *Proceedings of the DOE Chemical Energy Storage and Hydrogen Energy Systems Contracts Review,* prepared for the DOE by Jet Propulsion Laboratory, JPL Publication 78-1 (Pasadena, Cal.: Jet Propulsion Laboratory, California Institute of Technology, 1978), pp. 267–272.

page 57: AIR POLLUTANTS FROM BURNING METHANE OR HYDROGEN: Small amounts of nitrogen oxides (NO_x) and unburned hydrocarbon would be released by burning these fuels, especially when they were combusted in cogenerating engines, but these fuels burn much more cleanly than the liquid fuels now in use, and hence air pollution would be greatly reduced. In addition, it would be possible to control NO_x output from cogenerating engines either by redesigning them to operate at lower compression ratios and temperatures, or by using a catalytic converter on the exhaust stream.

page 59: METHANE GENERATED FROM MANURE IN OKLAHOMA: The Guymon, Oklahoma, project is described by C. W. Meckert, "The Calorific Project," in proceedings of Great Plains Extension Seminar and Tour, *Methane Production from Livestock Manure,* compiled by J. M. Sweeten (College Station, Tex.: Texas Agricultural Extension Service, Texas A & M University System; February 15, 1978), pp. 102–107. The price and quantity of methane sold from this project was obtained in a telephone conversation with Ron James, Marketing Director, Thermonetics, Inc., March 9, 1979.

page 59: THE 1979 PRICE OF NEW NATURAL GAS: See *The New York Times,* November 18, 1978.

page 59: BRITISH BOOK ON COGENERATORS, QUOTATION: R. M. E. Diamant, *Total Energy* (Oxford: Pergamon Press, 1970), p. vii. See pages 361–404 for descriptions of the U.S. cogenerator installations that are cited here.

page 60: METHANE FROM SEWAGE FOR THE STARRETT CITY HOUSING DEVELOPMENT: See *The Energy Daily* 6 (162), August 22, 1978, pp. 2–3.

page 60: MANHATTAN BUILDING HOPING TO SWITCH TO COGENERATION: See *The New York Times,* June 20, 1978. The trouble with using diesel fuel in an urban cogenerator is that it is now known that diesel engine exhaust contains significant concentration of carcinogens, adding to the already troublesome urban air-pollution problems. EPA has warned producers and users of diesel engines about this problem and is actively studying it.

page 60: THE TOTEM SYSTEM: See F. P. Ausiello et al., *TOTEM Total Energy Module,* cited above.

page 60: COST OF A TOTEM UNIT: Provided through a personal communication from the U.S. representative of the Fiat Corporation, December 1978.

page 62: THE AMOUNT OF NATURAL GAS NEEDED FOR THE SOLAR TRANSITION SCHEME: Mr. Robert Scott of the CBNS staff has worked out how a fifty-year scheme for the gradual introduction of various solar sources would affect the demand for various conventional sources of energy over that period of time. The scheme is described in some detail in testimony presented by Barry Commoner before the Environment, Energy and Natural Resources Subcommittee of the House Committee on Government Operations, in hearings on "The Administration's Solar Energy Policy," June 13, 1978 (cited above in note for p. 28). This testimony includes a diagram showing how conventional fuel consumption would be displaced by solar energy sources during the fifty-year transition (p. 29), and the amount of natural gas required was determined from this figure.

page 62: NATURAL GAS IN FORMATIONS NOW BEING TAPPED: See B. M. Miller, *Geological Estimates of Undiscovered Recoverable Oil and Gas Resources in the United States,* U.S. Geological Survey Circular 725 (Reston, Va.: U.S. Geological Survey, National Center, 1975), p. 34.

page 62: GEOPRESSURIZED METHANE: See M. H. Dorfman, "The Supply of Natural Gas from Geopressurized Zones: Engineering and Costs," in *The Future Supply of Nature-Made Petroleum and Gas, Technical Reports,* edited by R. F. Meyer, proceedings of a UNITAR Conference held in Schloss Laxenberg, Austria, in July 1976 (New York: Pergamon Press, 1977), pp. 873–911.

page 62: GAS FROM TIGHT FORMATIONS IN APPALACHIA: See Congressional Office of Technology Assessment, *Gas Potential from Devonian Shales of the Appalachian Basin* (Washington, D.C.: U.S. Government Printing Office, November 1977).

page 62: NEW TECHNIQUE FOR PRODUCING GAS FROM TIGHT FORMATIONS: See B. Hodgson, "Natural Gas: The Search Goes On," *National Geographic* 145 (6), November 1978, pp. 632–651. This article summarizes some of the new information about "unconventional" sources of natural gas. One of the ironic sidelights in this matter is that an earlier effort to release gas from tight formations by setting off an underground nuclear explosion (Project "Gas Buggy," part of an AEC effort to put a peaceful face on nuclear weaponry) failed. (Very little gas was released, and that was radioactive.) The new technique uses simple hydraulic pressure—a much more appropriate form of energy for the task than a nuclear blast.

page 62: MEETING OF GAS INDUSTRY EXPERTS: See R. H. Hefner III, "Presentation to the Panel on Future of Conventional U.S. Natural Gas Supplies—Quantification of conventional U.S. natural gas reserves and resources as a function of geographical location, depth and wellhead price; supply elasticity models and impact of regulatory policy" (Oklahoma City: The GHK Company, June 25–29, 1978). Mr. Hefner's company is very active in producing gas from tight formation and has amassed a good deal of information on the potential amounts available, and on production costs.

page 62: SURVEY OF LITERATURE ON U.S. NATURAL GAS RE-SOURCES: The following articles were used as the basis for estimating total gas resources in the U.S.: "The Supply of Natural Gas from Geopressurized Zones" (cited above) gave an estimate of 5,700 trillion cubic feet (TCF) of economically recoverable geopressurized methane. The OTA report, *Gas Potential from Devonian Shales of the Appalachian Basin* (cited above), stated that 23 to 35 TCF of methane can be recovered from the Appalachian tight formations. M. Deul and A. G. Kimm, "Coal Beds: A Source of Natural Gas," *The Oil and Gas Journal,* June 16, 1975, estimated that 300 TCF could be recovered from coal beds. Conventional resources of 900–1300 TCF were reported in *Geological Estimates of Undiscovered Recoverable Oil and Gas Resources in the United States* (cited above). Thus the total of these four estimates is 6923 to 7335 TCF. The cost of producing this gas was also obtained from these references.

page 63: LAND AREA REQUIREMENTS FOR SOLAR COLLECTORS AND PHOTOVOLTAIC CELLS: According to Saunders Miller (*The Economics of Nuclear and Coal Power,* cited above), about 1 kw (peak) of sunlight falls on the average square yard of land in the U.S., at noon on a sunny day. In an average year, a total of about 1,576 kWh of sunshine will fall on this square yard of land, or about 18 percent of the peak power, averaged over the 8,760 hours in a year. There are roughly 11,200 billion square yards of land in the U.S. In 1976 about 53 quads of oil, coal, and gas were consumed directly (other than for electricity production), or the equivalent of 15,675 billion kWh of electricity. Assuming that solar collectors operate at about 20 percent efficiency (a low figure, which would include periods in which the collector is not needed), about 50 billion square yards (16,100 square miles) of land would be required to generate an equivalent amount of heat energy. In 1976 the U.S. consumed 2,037 billion kWh of electricity (*Statistical Abstract,* 1978). It would require about 13 billion square yards (about 4,200 square miles) of photovoltaic cells, operating at 10 percent efficiency (i.e., generating 157.6 kWh per year per square yard), to produce this much electricity. 4,200 and 16,100 square miles of land represent .12 percent and .44 percent of the total U.S. land area, respectively.

page 64: MR. CARTER'S ANNOUNCEMENT ON THE CLINCH RIVER PROJECT: See *The Energy Daily,* 5 (69), April 8, 1977, pp. 1, 3. The attitude of environmentalists—or at least their representatives in Washington—toward the Carter energy plan was very much influenced by this announcement. By the time the Plan was announced, it had widespread support among Washington environmentalists and many of them signed a letter of support. However, just before the letter was to be released, at an informal meeting of these groups, Ralph Nader and I argued that because of its numerous faults (especially those described in the earlier chapters), the Plan did not merit support. The letter was never released, but someone forgot to inform Schlesinger of the change and he announced the release of the letter. His office later retracted the announcement.

page 64: The National Energy Plan QUOTATION: See *The National Energy Plan,* cited above.

page 64: O'LEARY QUOTATION: See *Solar Energy Intelligence Report,* October 30, 1978, 4 (43), p. 333.

page 64: CARTER QUOTATION: "Statement by the President," dated November 4, 1978, on the signing of H.R. 12874, "The Solar Photovoltaic Energy Research, Development, and Demonstration Act of 1978" (Washington, D.C.: Office of the White House Press Secretary, November 6, 1978).

7 THE HISTORIC PASSAGE: The Politics of Energy

page 66: MEXICO'S RESERVES: See, for example, *The Energy Daily,* 6 (239), December 14, 1978, pp. 1–10.

page 66: "THIS LARGE PRICE HIKE . . .": See *The New York Times,* December 18, 1978.

page 66: BYRD QUOTATION: See the Congressional Record, 125 (9), January 31, 1979, p. S 847; and the Washington *Post,* January 28, 1979.

page 69: FARMERS' INTERESTS IN ENERGY POLICY: See Barry Commoner, "Energy and Rural America" (cited above in note for p. 41).

page 69: LABOR'S INTERESTS IN ENERGY POLICY: For a detailed discussion of this issue see Barry Commoner, "Energy and Jobs," *Canadian Labour,* March 1978, paper presented at the Conference on Jobs and the Environment, Canadian Labour Council, Ottawa, Canada, February 20, 1978.

page 70: WESTINGHOUSE SUGGESTION THAT THE GOVERNMENT BUY NUCLEAR PLANTS: See L. J. Carter, "Nuclear Power: Westinghouse Looks to Washington for a Customer," *Science* 189 (4196), July 4, 1975, pp. 29–30.

page 70: ADMINISTRATION ATTEMPTS TO LIMIT ENVIRONMENTAL OBJECTIONS TO NUCLEAR PLANTS: See, for example, *The New York Times,* November 13, 1977. The administration has been trying, unsuccessfully thus far, to get a bill through Congress that will speed the construction of nuclear power plants.

page 71: RISING UTILITY RATES IN THE FACE OF FALLING DEMAND: See, for example, the response of New York City's Consolidated Edison Company to the proposal by a large building owner to begin cogenerating heat and electricity on site, as described in *The New York Times,* June 20, 1978 (cited above, note to p. 60).

page 71: DOUGHERTY'S ESTIMATES OF OIL INDUSTRY HOLDINGS IN COAL AND URANIUM: Quoted in an article, "Government Frets over Oil Moves into Nonoil Energy," in *The Oil and Gas Journal,* November 13, 1978, p. 106.

page 71: MANY U.S. GAS PRODUCERS ARE SMALL INDEPENDENTS: According to Jack Allen, president of the Independent Petroleum Association of America (IPAA), independent producers "drill 90% of the exploratory wells in the country" (*The Energy Daily,* February 20, 1979, p. 3). It is also interesting to note that Allen suggests that the number of operating drilling rigs in the U.S. dropped by 12 percent in the U.S. after the passage of the Natural Gas Policy Act, a clear response to the fact that the bill makes it more profitable to leave gas in the ground than to produce it.

page 72: CURRENT TRENDS IN THE OIL INDUSTRY: The quotations are from an article by B. Tippee, "Management Takes Steps to Adapt to Big Changes," *The Oil and Gas Journal,* November 13, 1978, pp. 105–111. The article also summarizes recent oil company investments in other areas.

page 72: MAJOR OIL COMPANY QUOTATION: The quotations are from an article by R. Sumpter, "U.S. Producers Caught in Cost/Price Squeeze," *The Oil and Gas Journal,* December 4, 1978, pp. 23–27. This article develops the theme of the earlier *Oil and Gas Journal* article, cited above.

page 72: SWERINGEN QUOTATION: See the Chicago *Tribune,* April 19, 1978.

page 72: OIL COMPANY PROFIT RATES WOULD HAVE DROPPED TO 2 PERCENT BY 1985: According to the National Petroleum Council study, *U.S. Energy Outlook: Oil and Gas Availability* (Washington, D.C.: National Petroleum Council, 1973), cited above: "In 1985, the rate of return on net fixed assets would decline to a completely unacceptable level of about 2 percent" (p. 71).

page 73: OIL COMPANY ADVERTISING CAMPAIGNS: The greatest effort seems to have been made by the Mobil Corporation, which publishes frequent advertisements that blame most of the energy problems on government regulations, price controls, and environmental requirements. The advertisements leave a reader with the distinct impression that despite the numerous difficulties in the field of energy, the oil companies, unlike the government or environmentalists, have made no mistakes.

page 75: ELECTRIC UTILITIES' POSSESSING 50 PERCENT MORE SURPLUS CAPACITY: According to the National Electric Reliability Council's *8th Annual Review of Overall Reliability and Adequacy of the North American Bulk Power Systems* (Princeton, N.J.: National Electric Reliability Council, August 1978), the total peak (summer) demand for electricity in the U.S. in 1977 was 387,255 million watts. The total installed generating capacity was 506,193 million watts, which amounts to more than a 30 percent reserve margin. However, normal utility practice requires only a 20 percent reserve margin, according to the Bank-

ers Trust Company, *Energy Viewpoint, U.S. Electric Power—Will It Be Reliable Enough?* (New York: Bankers Trust Company, November 1978). Thus U.S. utilities had about 41,500 million watts of unused and unneeded capacity in 1977 or more than 10 percent of their total peak demand.

page 75: "THE ROOT PROBLEM . . .": See *The New York Times,* January 31, 1979.

page 76: The New York Times QUOTATION: See *The New York Times,* October 24, 1976.

page 76: Wall Street Journal QUOTATION: See *Wall Street Journal,* October 27, 1976.

page 76: MORGAN QUOTATION: See James Morgan, *Our Presidents,* 3rd ed. (Toronto: The Macmillan Company, 1969), p.127.

page 76: HIDDEN ISSUE IN THE 1976 CAMPAIGN: For a more detailed discussion of the parallels between the politics of the "ignominious era" and the 1976 campaign, see Barry Commoner, "A New Historic Passage: Energy, the Economy, and the Era of Constraints," in Baron (ed.), *The National Purpose Reconsidered* (New York: Columbia University Press, 1978), pp. 53–72.

page 76: CARTER PRESS CONFERENCE QUOTATIONS: See *The New York Times,* January 30, 1979.

page 77: RATE OF PROFIT ON FOREIGN AND DOMESTIC OIL OPERATIONS: H. W. Blauvelt described the rates of profit on foreign and domestic oil operations in "How to Become a Foreign Oil Company," in *Exploration and Economics of the Petroleum Industry* (Houston, Tex.: Gulf Publishing Company, 1966), p. 273. Blauvelt's article includes a graph which demonstrates that from 1950 to 1957 the U.S. oil companies' rate of return on equity in foreign operations remained above 25 percent, while the comparable figure for domestic operations averaged around 12 percent. See also Commoner, *The Poverty of Power,* cited above, p. 62.

page 77: KENTUCKIAN'S VIEW OF VIRGINIA: As quoted in Allan Nevins, *Ordeal of the Union,* Vol. 1 (New York: Charles Scribner's Sons, 1947), p. 462.

page 77: ALLAN NEVINS ON POLITICIANS' AND BUSINESSMEN'S VIEWS: See *Ordeal of the Union,* Vol. 2, p. 242, cited above.

page 78: HELLER QUOTATION: See *U.S. News & World Report,* November 27, 1978, p. 66. For further discussion of the decline in innovation, see "Experts Upset by Drop in Innovative Research," *The New York Times,* May 31, 1978.

page 78: The New York Times QUOTATION: See *The New York Times,* July 10, 1977.

page 79: POWER PLANTS PRODUCE MORE EFFICIENTLY THAN TWENTY YEARS AGO: See Bruce A. Smith, *Technological Innovation in Electric Power Generation 1950–1970* (East Lansing, Mich.: Michigan State University, Graduate School of Business Administration, 1977).

page 80: ALLAN NEVINS ON FRANKLIN PIERCE'S INAUGURAL ADDRESS: See *Ordeal of the Union,* Vol. 2, p. 45, cited above.

page 80: CARTER QUOTATION: See Jimmy Carter, *A Government as Good as Its People* (New York: Pocket Books, 1978), p. 253. This is a collection of Mr. Carter's campaign speeches, ending with his inaugural address, which is quoted in the text.

page 80: ALLAN NEVINS ON ELECTIONS OF 1852: See *Ordeal of the Union,* Vol. 2, p. 3, cited above.

page 80: VOTER TURNOUT IN ELECTIONS OF 1960 AND 1976: See *Statistical Abstract,* 1978, p. 520, cited above.

page 80: CITIZEN QUOTATION: See *The New York Times,* October 26, 1976.

page 81: "POLITICS OF AUSTERITY": See *Newsweek,* January 29, 1979.

page 81: "THE DECLINE OF U.S. POWER": See *Business Week,* March 12, 1979.

Acknowledgments

Much of the information and ideas on which this book is based is derived from work carried on by my colleagues of the staff of the Center for the Biology of Natural Systems at Washington University. I am particularly indebted to Rob Scott for his clear-cut analyses of the numerical intricacies of the National Energy Plan and their convoluted relationship to the PIES model, for preparing the Notes for this book, for tracking down and checking the relevant data, and for his many other contributions; to Richard Carlson for his patient and illuminating discussion of economic questions; to David Friedman, who, together with Richard Carlson and Rob Scott, has been analyzing the promising ways of improving the relationships between agriculture and the energy system; and to Jim Kendell and David Kriebel, who, with all of the foregoing, have so liberally shared their thoughts and enthusiasm for the subject with me. In the preparation of the manuscript, I have had the valuable assistance of Jacqueline Zinner, who carefully assembled much of the material for the Notes; of Elizabeth Powers, who typed a good deal of the early drafts; and of Jennifer Hoppe, who gave many hours of her very considerable skills to the preparation of the manuscript. And for their many incisive contributions to the development of the ideas expressed in this book I owe considerably to my good friends Allan Brotsky, Piero Dolara, and Alan McGowan. Finally I wish to thank Lisa Feiner, whose warm yet wise and critical interest made the task of writing this book much more rewarding than it might have been. As ever, the staff at Knopf, Bob Gottlieb, Kathy Hourigan, and Martha Kaplan, have done a remarkably effective job in bringing this project to fruition.

Index

A NOTE ON THE TYPE

The text of this book was set by computer in a face called Primer,
designed by Rudolph Ruzicka, earlier responsible for the design of
Fairfield and Fairfield Medium, Linotype faces whose virtues have for
some time now been accorded wide recognition.

The complete range of sizes of Primer was first made available in
1954, although the pilot size of 12 point was ready as early as 1951. The
design of the face makes general reference to Linotype Century (long a
serviceable type, totally lacking in manner or frills of any kind) but
brilliantly corrects the characterless quality of that face.

Composed by The Haddon Craftsmen, Inc., Scranton, Pennsylvania.
Printed and bound by American Book–Stratford Press, Saddle Brook,
New Jersey.
Typography and binding design by Virginia Tan.